Inner Child

Rediscover Your Worth Overcoming the Shadows

(Take Back Control of Your Life Immediately and Reach Your Full Potential)

Kerry Daniels

Published By **Tyson Maxwell**

Kerry Daniels

All Rights Reserved

Inner Child: Rediscover Your Worth Overcoming the Shadows (Take Back Control of Your Life Immediately and Reach Your Full Potential)

ISBN 978-1-7775324-7-5

No part of this guidebook shall be reproduced in any form without permission in writing from the publisher except in the case of brief quotations embodied in critical articles or reviews.

Legal & Disclaimer

The information contained in this book is not designed to replace or take the place of any form of medicine or professional medical advice. The information in this book has been provided for educational & entertainment purposes only.

The information contained in this book has been compiled from sources deemed reliable, and it is accurate to the best of the Author's knowledge; however, the Author cannot guarantee its accuracy and validity and cannot be held liable for any errors or omissions. Changes are periodically made to this book. You must consult your doctor or get professional medical advice before using any of the suggested remedies, techniques, or information in this book.

Upon using the information contained in this book, you agree to hold harmless the Author from and against any damages, costs, and expenses, including any legal fees potentially resulting from the application of any of the information provided by this guide. This disclaimer applies to any damages or injury caused by the use and application, whether directly or indirectly, of any advice or information presented, whether for breach of contract, tort, negligence, personal injury, criminal intent, or under any other cause of action.

You agree to accept all risks of using the information presented inside this book. You need to consult a professional medical practitioner in order to ensure you are both able and healthy enough to participate in this program.

Table Of Contents

Chapter 1: Echoes Of A Fragile Past 1

Chapter 2: The Footprints Of Feet In The Sand 13

Chapter 3: A Dance Of Grace 26

Chapter 4: Gentle Warriors 39

Chapter 5: A Heart's Journey To Wholeness" 53

Chapter 6: Tears That Changed Us 73

Chapter 7: Whispers Of Solace 87

Chapter 8: Talking About The Childhood Trauma 115

Chapter 9: The Three Parts Of Trauma. 122

Chapter 10: Childhood Have On Adults 128

Chapter 11: Recognizing The Signs Of Trauma 135

Chapter 12: The Seven Healing Stages . 142

Chapter 13: The 3 Steps To Beating Childhood Trauma 147

Chapter 14: The Consequences Of Not Recovering 155

Chapter 15: Looking For Greater Happiness And Health 164

Chapter 16: Finding Solace In Faith 173

Chapter 1: Echoes Of A Fragile Past

"Unveiling the Veiled Scars: The Tender Heartbreak of Innocence Lost"

In the hidden recesses of my memory, where the memories of the past are tucked away in the air like gentle breezes, am able to retrace the steps of my youth--a path that traces softly the path that is woven by darkness as well as the light. It was there, deep in the shadows of childhood, I experienced the aching acceptance of pain and etched its footprint on the surface of my heart as a young one.

My tale, as many others, starts by shedding the tears of innocence gone. The glorious times of youth, the world seemed like a dazzling tapestry, with threads of wonder, laughter and fantasies that seemed unending. There was a magical world unspoiled, and each moment was ablaze with the brightness of thousands of stars.

Then fate, despite hidden motives did not have any other ideas in for the future.

With the flick in a second, the vivid shades of my childhood's canvas were gone and I was thrown into the darkest reaches of my soul which I never understood. There, memories of my fragile past began to echo, an orchestra of hurt, uncertainty and vulnerability, which echoed in my heart.

The tenderness of the petals as they shivered against an unstoppable storm My innocence was washed off, leaving scars which would be hidden from people around the globe. My heart, previously an oasis of joy and unending love, turned into an insecure vessel that carried the weight of feelings I was unable to comprehend. The world that was once so appealing, suddenly seemed a bit hazy and unforgiving.

The days following I was able to master how to wear an elaborate mask, one that is created to protect us from the chaos within.

Being afraid of being seen as damaged, broken or strange led me to cover my suffering in a smile, laughter, and a confident face. However, what a heavy burden I felt in my tender heart! The tears I was afraid to shed gathered like raindrops that had been forgotten, creating an invisible ocean of emotion which threatened to consume me.

The experience of childhood trauma can be described as an adventure of inexplicably painful struggles and symphonies of quiet fights that took place within the spaces of one's own soul. Every step was as if I was walking on pieces of glass. Yet I fought, determined to discover the strength needed to overcome the pain that was threatening to swallow my whole.

When I was in the shadows I was longing for some light that could guide me, a flicker of hope to guide me along the maze of my feelings. It was in this barren environment that I uncovered the roots of resilience fragile and delicate, yet determined in their search for to survive. The realization that I wasn't the only one as others also weighed the burden of concealed wounds that gave hope into the flames of optimism within me.

Then I began to unravel my layers of heart and gently peel back my protective shield I created with great care. As I embraced vulnerability I found the courage to confront my past to confront those fears that held me in a cage. When I let myself be vulnerable, and heal, I realized that the ghosts of the past need not define me. They were just aspect of the vast weave of my existence.

The chapter you are reading of my book, dear reader, isn't only a retelling of my own tale, it is a testimony to the strength and resilience inside each of us. This chapter is a look into the heartbreak and tenderness that accompany losing innocence and the scars hidden from view that form the outline of our hearts. The vulnerability that lies beneath is a tremendous one that is born from accepting the fragments of our fragile history, recognizing the trauma as well as embarking on the path to self-recovery and healing.

In the vibrant tapestry of my youth the harmonies of dreams and laughter created an enchanting symphony and the world was ablaze with endless delight. But, underneath the bright colors, a shadow hung in the air-- a dimness that could be a threat to the essence of the person I was.

The story of my life took a surprising twist, bringing me into an area that was a blur of innocence, when innocence came into conflict with the adversities. My once-sonic symphony early years was suddenly disrupted and being replaced by a sombre recollection of my fragile history.

The pain of the loss of innocence created a devastating map of my youthful soul with hidden wounds which were not visible to anyone else. The world that was once warm and welcoming, has now become as a vast uncharted area, filled with mysterious threats.

As the aftermath of the upheaval raged on and turmoil, I found myself in unknown terrains, trying to navigate the maze of alleyways of grieving. My heart, previously an oasis of joy and unending love was weighed down by emotions that were beyond my understanding.

In fear of rejection and judgment In the face of rejection and judgment, I sought refuge by hiding behind a mask, a cloak of smiles and laughter that concealed the turmoil in. However, the uncut emotional elation and shame accumulated in a steady tidal wave, that were threatening to overwhelm me.

The experience of childhood trauma was an edgy odyssey that was laced by silent struggle--a battle within that I fought with courage as well as fear. Every step was as if I was dancing at the edge uncertain and tense but I fought in the same determination.

Through the darkness, a glimpse of hope arose, a light that promised reconciliation and healing. Within the fellowship of people who faced their personal fears, and embraced their weaknesses as I did, I discovered solace as well as a glimpse of the possibility of hope.

As I shivered and exuberantly waited I began peeling off the layers that comprised my heart, opening my hidden scars and revealing them to the illumination of compassion and understanding. A gentle journey to healing began, bringing a fresh feeling of power--a strength that sprung through the cracks of my heart. I was able to see an enduring heart.

The ghosts of my fragile past did not frighten me anymore and became a part of the music that defined my life. Each note of healing as well as discovery grew, blending the pain and hope.

I'd like to invite you into my deepest soul, a view of my tapestry, that is woven from experiences and feelings and infused with darkness and light. We embark together in a voyage through the triumphs and tragedies of childhood traumas, as they've shaped us into the resilient creatures that we have become today.

This book should serve as an affirmation that even when we are shattered by the loss of innocence, we are blessed with an inborn strength, a unstoppable energy that can ignite the fires of renewal and healing. When we travel through the lands of vulnerability, we can be able to find common ground in the lives of other people who have walked the same path, creating an orchestra of strength and bravery that resonates in the soul.

Within the bustling city that is New York, there lived one girl who was known as Patricia. The home she once enjoyed was now a battlefield due to her mother's Catherine was the victim of domestic violence sparked by her father Thomas. The alcohol-fueled Thomas's fury unleashed an unstoppable fury on the family.

Patricia's childhood was spent tripping over eggshells and living in the fear of her father's violent outbursts. The walls around their house contained the secrets of a night filled with tears and broken fantasies. The darkness of Patricia's heart was filled with terror and hatred--a flurry of emotion that was unstoppable.

A fateful evening that night, the weather reached a tragic peak, culminating with the tragic loss of her beloved mother Catherine. Her loss of anchor caused Patricia lost, her heart broken, and her heart broken irreparably. Devastated by grief and the weight of unresolved feelings, she was struggling to breathe in the wake of the tragedy.

When Patricia became an adult The shadows of her childhood refused to let go of their hold. Trauma-related echoes hung around her with a relentless stream of specters, reminding her of her suffering. Within her relationships, she was struggling to be able to trust others and allow them into her world, afraid that the vulnerability could only cause greater heartbreak.

In a state of denial over the events of her youth, Patricia yearned to break away from the tethers of her childhood. The story of Chapter 1 was a reflection of her struggles, a moving account of the loss of innocence as well as the tender pain that remains in the aftermath of her darkest moments.

To heal herself, Patricia embarked on a transformational journey. She sought out the help of counsellors and groups of support and was determined to face those demons which had afflicted her for a long time. Every step she smashed back the layers of hurt and allowed herself to mourn over the death of her mom as well as the time that was taken away from her by the violent acts.

Through the abyss of therapy Patricia discovered that she could not bear the weight of his father's sinnings. The act of forgiveness was not the same as accepting his conduct; instead it was an moment of release, a liberation from the tangles of hatred which had encircled her heart.

In the process of rebuilding her life Patricia realized her strength and determination. She turned her grief into advocacy, and acted as the voice of those who suffered silently. Through each act of kindness and compassion, she was able to find the healing she needed not only for herself and her family, but also for those around her too.

Patricia's story is a one of a woman who was amidst the most harrowing of storms, and came out with a heart of love and strength. My traumatic childhood have helped shape my present self-image, proving that, even in the midst of unimaginable suffering recovery and transformation are achievable.

By sharing my story in this blog, I would like to help people who have also walked similar roads. The process of healing isn't linear, it's an ongoing procedure, with a variety of changes and ups. It is only by embracing vulnerability and self-compassion you can find the strength needed to face the dark shadows which haunt us.

Chapter 2: The Footprints Of Feet In The Sand

"Carrying the Weight of Shadows: Navigating the Path of Healing"

In the immense expanse of time, the traces of my life stretch across the sands of time. Much like delicate traces in sand, they reveal the story of a youthful soul who was once dancing in the sunshine of childhood but was soon drenched in the dark shadows of mental trauma. Every step that is etched into the sand acts as an ode to the burden I carried, a burden that sometimes, could keep me in dark for the rest of my life.

When I was a kid I was a delicate ship, traversing in uncharted waters, with huge love for my family and a desire to be safe. Within the walls of my family home, violent storms of addiction and violence took over, leaving my heart battered and my heart broken.

As the grief of loss grew the steps I took slowed down in the wake of loss, leaving me to search for my way through the shifting sands and dune of grief and desperation. I buried within me thoughts of hatred and fear at the very person that was once meant to love and protect me. The pain and uncertainty which seized my heart was constant, making me in the grips of self-doubt, self-blame and self-pity.

However, in my worst of moments, I saw that the sand underneath my feet remained the mark of perseverance--a testament to my resilient spirit that inspired me to continue moving ahead, regardless of what the path may be uncertain. Each step was weighed down by shadows. But I also saw the sparks of optimism, light-colored rays which whispered about the possibilities of renewal and healing.

Healing journeys are an intricate journey, in which every step mirrored the fight for a firm foundation amid the sands that shift in trauma. It was a journey to self-discovery and the delicate dance of keeping the past in mind and aspiring for the hope of a brighter tomorrow.

When I was adolescent, the footprints that sand left led me on a journey of my identity, a process of reuniting parts of me that had been smashed through the storm. I sought refuge within the arms of my people who, as lights in the darkness they reminded me that I wasn't restricted by the shadows of my history.

My footprints started to appear and morph into an intricate pattern of strength and strength, which is a testament of my capacity to rise over the raging waves of life. My fragile past did not serve just as a reminder the pain, but also an inspiration for wisdom and understanding, prompting me to be compassionate to people who had to carry the burden of their own.

As I grew older, my footprints left in the sand remained to guide me through life, when I negotiated relationships shaped by the experiences of my childhood. The battle to be confident and accept vulnerability was not over and yet, with the support of a community of souls who understood I discovered a place in which healing flourished.

In looking back over my footprints that I left behind, I saw that my path to healing wasn't one-way. It was an intricate dance of flows and changes, that saw triumphs and setbacks coexist creating a portrait of strength that sparkled like a glimmer in the rough sands of life.

These footsteps are not only mine, but are an expression of the global experience of healing through childhood trauma. While you follow me in this little odyssey I pray that you can find comfort in the knowledge that every step, however it may seem a little unsure it is part of the orchestra of strength and optimism.

In my journey of healing, the footprints left in the sand uncovered the development of my personal story--a tale woven through the threads of strength in the face of vulnerability, self-discovery, and courage. The footprints that were left behind mirror my many times when I faced the turbulent waves of my life and made the decision to overcome their constant pull.

Within the warm embrace of a therapy session, I set off on an introspection journey by carefully following the footsteps of the trauma I experienced in my childhood. Through tear-stained confessions, and confessed truths, my mind was able to confront my ghosts from the past by exposing the trauma that I'd hid from for too long.

As each day passed I saw the footprints of sandy soil transform into symbols of forgiveness and resilience. Shadows weighed less as I found the strength to face the hatred I held for my father. The walls I'd erected around me began to crumble, unveiling an open heart that longed to break free of the burdens of anger.

The footprints of the sand weaved a web of development and a testimony to my unstoppable determination to find my own identity. When I was grieving over my mother who had passed away and also cherished her life, which carried in the warmth of my memory. After the devastation of my mother's death I saw the sparks of the hope of a bright flame that guided me to a new tomorrow that promised of recovery.

But, as with the constantly shifting the sands under my feet, my journey was not effortless. There were moments where the burden of my past was threatening to take me over at times, and I felt like I was being pulled back to the darkness that I tried to get out of. However, with every step, I realized I was able to hold my ground in the turmoil and to reclaim the story of my story.

The footprints on the sand were evidence of my moments of extending forgiveness, not just for the sake of my father, instead for my own freedom. With forgiveness, I gained liberation from the ties of resentment which tied me to my previous. This was a sign of self-love and a decision to let go of being a victim and to embrace the strength of the resilience.

When I continued on the road I met those who'd walked their own personal deserts of grief. Their eyes could see reflections of my hurt, and within their tales, I found the comfort of. As a group, we built the strength of a group, a unwavering assistance system that carried us through some of the toughest circumstances.

The footprints of the sand guided me toward the goal of my life, leading me to speak out for change and give my voice to those who have been silenced through violence. Through my activism, I discovered the feeling of being empowered, which allowed me to transform my grief into something bigger, and to make a permanent mark in the world.

When I open this chapter for you to read, I share that I am Patricia, the bearer of footprints in sandy ground, and a victim of childhood trauma. My tale, as many other stories, is a tangled weaving of healing and pain that combines light and shadows. As I danced with vulnerability, I found that I had the power to conquer my most difficult times and come out from my experiences with a heart full of love.

Here I am now and now, not as a reminder of my own past, but rather as an example of the strength that is inside us all. The footprints of the sand led me to an important realization: it is possible to heal, that it is possible to grow in love, and that both forgiveness and love have the ability to heal even the most traumatic scars.

When we embark on this adventure together, let us take comfort from each other's footprints, and the strength that unites us all as survivors. As a group, we travel hand in hand and leave behind footprints of hope and courage in the direction of an era that is filled with hope of transformation and healing.

The final chapter in "Footprints in the Sand," I'm feeling overwhelmed by emotions, because this process of healing and self-discovery is profoundly transformative. Every step I've taken through the shifting sands that have been carved by trauma have shaped me into who I am today, a survivor an ally and a source of optimism.

My footprints on the sand bear witness to the struggles of carrying the burden of shadows to moments of terror and hatred could have sucked my soul. However, even in the middle dark, I realized the power that is in each one of us - the resilience built from vulnerability, and the ability for compassion that can heal the most traumatic hurts.

When we go through our lives leaving behind the imprint of our experiences, a collage of experiences that have changed our lives. Like the way that tides wash away any footprints that are left on the sand of time, life also provides us with the chance to reinvent ourselves, transcend the past and accept the possibility of a better tomorrow.

For those following a similar route, I have some words of wisdom It is not a lonely journey. The path you take is entirely yours and it holds the opportunity for change and development. The footprints that you leave behind will tell a story - a tale of bravery, resilience and of optimism. Take the lessons from your history and don't allow them to be the sole reason for your life. Instead, consider them an opportunity to build a new life that's truly yours.

The journey to healing is not about a specific destination and is rather a journey that calls us to spread compassion and empathy not only towards others, but also us. Keep your eyes on yourself when you traverse the muddy terrain of grief, for in the heart there is a reservoir of strength awaiting to be discovered.

Rely on the belief that the past that are a bit of a blur have to determine your destiny. Like footprints that are left in sandy soil are removed as well, the burden of shadows lift off your soul. Within your vulnerability is the ability to turn pain to compassion, fear into strength, and hatred to forgiveness.

Keep faith in the belief that you're in a position to conquer whatever difficulties could befall you. Offer your support to others who can offer help, as the connection is where provides comfort and power. Be aware that healing isn't the sole journey of healing it is made with the support and compassion of those who have been on similar journeys.

While we are preparing to begin the journey together take the lessons learned from this story in our souls. The footprints left in the sand continue to lead us and remind us of the beautiful things that emerges from even difficult situations.

We can take comfort by knowing that the footprints we leave, no however small they may be, will leave a lasting impression as a evidence of our perseverance as well as our progress and our relentless determination to take back our lives. Our journey isn't ending, yet with each move we make towards the healing and transformation that lies ahead of our feet.

I urge you to accept your own footprints on the sand and be able to see the beauty of their inertia, as they represent the path of someone who been through the dark and come out unharmed however, stronger and more sensitive than ever.

While we go in this Journey with one another, let us stroll hand-in-hand leaving the footprints of hope and strength in the direction of an era that is filled with the possibility of transformation and healing.

Let us stroll hand-in-hand leaving footprints on the sand and carrying the burden of our shadows while we accept the hope of healing as well as the power of the perseverance. Through the shifting sands that tell our lives, let us discover the power to stand tall above the waves of our past and leave an enduring legacy of love and compassion for our own lives and others who as well, are bearing the burden of their own footprints the sand.

Chapter 3: A Dance Of Grace

"Embracing the Broken Pieces: Unraveling the Tapestry of Self-Compassion"

In the mellow symphony of the healing process, Chapter 3 is the start of a graceful dance, in which I began to take in my broken pieces of soul, and then make them into an intricate tapestry of self-compassion. Every step in this intricate dance of self-discovery was an affirmation of the beautiful which can be uncovered from fragments from a broken past.

While I continued on the road of healing, I came to the crossroads, a point at which I was forced to face the effects that linger from my trauma from childhood. My fragile past were still echoing in me, however, amidst the hurt, I started to listen for the sounds of self-compassion, a soft melody that encouraged me to love me, and embrace my injuries with compassion rather than judgement.

The grace dance required enormous courage because it involved letting go of the cover of self-blame and self-criticism which became second nature. Every step was a learning experience as I was able to substitute the words of hate with words of compassion and affection. As I gazed into my reflection I could see not an unbroken soul however, but an individual with strength that was visible by the lines of endurance across her face.

The performance was not free of mistakes and stumbles. At times of vulnerability in the face of doubt, self-doubt were threatening to drag me into the depths of despair. The marks in the sand of my past appeared to be a constant threat, and I was left wondering if I really deserved to be able to heal and find happiness.

However, in the deepest part of my soul there was a seed of endurance that took root. The seed was that was nurtured by the echo of Chapter 1--a chapter which witnessed the courage required to face my past trauma. The seeds were nourished by the footprints left in Chapter 2--a chapter that showed me the importance of forgiveness and vulnerability.

When I danced my way through the corridors of my therapy, I realized that my value wasn't determined by the scars I've suffered from my past, but my strength in acknowledging my vulnerability. The grace dance became an invitation to accept the hurt of my former self, to wrap her in my arms with love as I reassured her that she was not blamed in the darkness that was engulfing her.

Each time I danced this dance changed my perception. Instead of seeing my history as an obligation to shoulder I started to see it as an opportunity to gain strength and wisdom, a testimony to my capability to overcome challenges. The self-compassion tapestry I weaved showed me that healing wasn't focused on erasing the past rather, it was about taking on all the aspects of my life--the broken pieces and the whole that is resilient.

With grace, I was able to find freedom - a escape from the burdens of self-doubt which had held me down for a long time. It wasn't about achieving an endpoint, but rather seeking beauty on the path, a journey to self-discovery and acceptance.

Dear reader As you continue to watch the grace dance, I encourage you to take me in this journey of self-love. The dance demands the courage to be vulnerable, brave, and the ability to accept the fractured pieces of our souls. Like the footprints that were left in the sand showed us how to overcome our previous experiences, the dance is a way to discover beauty in the sloppy actions we make on our journey.

Be aware that healing doesn't happen in a linear fashion but rather a dance. It's an never-ending journey that demands the patience and affection of a loving partner. Accept the grace dance by embracing it with a wide smile, as inside lies the transformational capacity of self-compassion, a force that is able to heal even the most damaged of souls.

The dance of grace was continuing, I felt wrapped in a feeling of love and acceptance, a warm hug that encompassed every inch of my existence. The self-compassion tapestry I weaved contained both times of joy and moments of struggle, reminding me that every move in the dance proved my strength.

As I danced I came to realize that healing did not mean erasing my wounds, but rather honouring the process that took my to the place I am in the present. The footprints on the sand of my life did not become an burden to be carried instead, they were a symbol of strength and progress--a evidence that I'd weathered the storms with hearts that were more loving and sensitive than I have ever had.

Each time I took a graceful step I was able to forgive myself for those times that I was weak, and for those times when I fell and lost my footing. It was clear that I am human, and within my imperfections was the beauty in imperfections. The dance of grace showed me it was acceptable to be a victim of scars, and bear the burden of shadows, because inside those scars were stories of strength and resilience.

The gentle rhythm of the dance, I mingled with others who were on their own paths to healing. We were a group bound with the belief that healing is not an individual endeavor. We held hands during the turns and twists of the dance and found strength from the support of others who understood.

As a group, we commemorate those milestones, the moments where self-love bloomed like a blossom on the sand. We rejoicing in the strength that was required to take every step, no matter the road was rocky. We also shared our vulnerability there was a sense of friendship that illuminated the darkest parts of our hearts.

The grace dance taught me to be deserving of kindness and love--not only from other people and from me, but also to myself. This realization made me want to nurture my own child tenderly by offering her the love and attention she so badly desired in her most difficult times.

I offer you an invitation to dance with me in this dance of grace that transcends those pages in this book and continues into the stunning world of your personal life. While you dance with compassion and grace May you gain confidence to accept your journey through all of the twists and turns realizing that your footprints on the sand will be a testimony to your tenacity.

With the soft movement of the dance we experience the transformational capacity of self-compassion, the ability to repair our damaged pieces and embrace ourselves in the unconditional love of our hearts. Dance may be difficult sometimes, but in the choreography is the key for liberation: freedom to forgive, recover, and find beauty within the mix in our daily lives.

In the course of our journey together, we should be grateful for our shortcomings, while acknowledging the fact that they're part of what makes us human. As we work together in harmony to achieve the healing of our community Let us seek solace in our strength, courage, and determination to weave a beautiful weaving of grace that is infused with hope and compassion. The dance of grace isn't just a personal tale; it's a song of perseverance that resonates in all of us.

The grace dance isn't a dance in the literal sense however, it's a metaphorical symbol of the path to healing. It is the graceful movements of self-compassion and forgiveness and acceptance in the course of navigating the twists and turns that come with our thoughts and life experiences. Like a graceful dancer who is fluid and poised and grace, the graceful dance encourages us to face our life's difficulties with a feeling of compassion and understanding toward ourselves as well as other people.

In the midst of this dance is the notion of self-compassion - the practice of taking care of ourselves with the same compassion and empathy as we'd extend to our dear friends. It's about acknowledging the fact that humans are creatures, and that as human beings, we have flaws and imperfections. By cultivating self-compassion we are able to accept our flaws and shortcomings, while acknowledging that they're part of what makes us human.

The dance of grace teaches people to shed the self-blame, self-doubt and blame. It's about getting rid of the stress of carrying the burden of our past, and accepting that we performed as best we could using the tools we were given when we were in that moment. The dance allows us to change our own story, changing our judgmental voices into ones of wisdom and compassion.

While swaying across the halls of therapy, I learned that the dance demands a lot of bravery. The dance requires us to confront our most painful hurts as well as the suffering that's been hidden from us for too many years. We are challenged to face the dark side of our history and find the courage to see the inner light in the midst of us.

The graceful dance does not come without a few blunders. It is not without its moments where self-doubt's shadows are threatening to plunge us in the dark and the footprints left by our past linger over our present. In those instances, we can find comfort by recognizing that dance isn't all about perfection but about moving forward.

Each time we take a graceful step We learn to accept moments when we felt vulnerable, and for those moments that we were unable to walk and fall. We acknowledge that we're capable of loving and caring regardless of any flaws or failures. It is an opportunity to remind ourselves that we are worthy of the same respect and compassion we extend to other people.

As I was held by grace I was able to confront my child with love. I gave her the love and tenderness she so longingly sought in the darkest times. The grace dance taught me that healing is not just about healing my wounds rather, it was about taking on all the aspects of me--the broken pieces as well as the resilient whole.

I offer you an invitation to dance with me in this show of grace. A dance that transcends the pages in this chapter and is extended to the vast landscape of your existence. Accept the steps that aren't perfect with the knowledge that they are an integral part of the transformational path to healing.

Within the context of this chapter The "dance of grace" is an evocative representation of the healing process and self-discovery the main character, Patricia, goes through on her way to overcome childhood trauma. The dance is symbolic of the delicate, transformational dance that she takes on when she begins to accept the past, manage her feelings, and discover compassion for herself.

"Grace" or "grace" in the dance signifies the qualities of grace, elegance and respect. It is the expression of compassion and forgiveness toward oneself as well as other people. The grace dance involves that you face challenges in life by exhibiting a certain degree of compassion and acceptance, even when faced with suffering and difficulties.

As a dance demands dancers with rhythm, the path of healing isn't linear. It is a journey that involves both periods of ups and downs, times of vulnerability and moments of victory. The dance of grace supports acceptance of the scars and imperfections as element of healing knowing that our events shape us into the person that we are.

The grace dance encapsulates the path of growth and healing by highlighting the splendor which emerges from the fragments of a broken past. This is a continual journey of self-discovery in which one is able to walk across the world with kindness empathy, and an open heart, creating a greater relationship with us and our surroundings.

In the midst of this journey in unity, let's be proud of our strength and the capacity to accept our flaws by loving. With the soft sway in the grace of our hearts, we are able to find comfort, and within the self-compassionate rhythm that is awe-inspiring and self-compassion, we discover the power to stitch the fragments of our lives into the fabric that is healing and hopeful.

Chapter 4: Gentle Warriors

"The Conquest of Tenderness: A Voyage of Fearless Hearts"

This Chapter reveals the heartwarming story of "Gentle Warriors"--a section dedicated to people, just like me who've fought the dark with a ferocious spirit and come out triumphant thanks to the strength of love and strength. This chapter celebrates the unstoppable nature of each of us, the warriors who traverse the battlefield of pain with hearts brimming with courage and compassion.

The path of a kind warrior isn't one of brutal force or violent battles. It is rather a way to transcend chaos and clamor and embraces vulnerability as armor and using compassion as an instrument. It's the triumph of love--a strength that speaks rather than yells and which heals, not damaging.

The heart of gentle warriors is the delicate power of strength. It comes from the core of our souls. It's the capacity to face the most traumatic memories, face the darkest shadows with open arms and accept those parts of us that are wounded in a gentle way. It's the strength to take the road towards healing even if you are surrounded by fear and anxiety.

With a group of gentle warriors, I realized the true meaning of sisterhood - a relationship that transcends the boundaries of time and space, created by the blazes of determination. Though we were at first strangers but our experiences together led us to become a community of like-minded people connected by a common thread of perseverance and a determination to take back our lives.

The calm and serenity that therapy provides We cultivated compassion for ourselves by being gentle to ourselves whenever the burden of our past was about to overwhelm our lives. This was no straightforward process, since we'd gotten used to self-criticism and harsh judgment, believing that love was a luxury we were unable to afford.

In the holy realm that is healing saw that tenderness wasn't an indicator of weakness but an expression of power. Hearts blossomed as delicate blossoms looking for the light of self-love. With each step we unveiled the armor layers which had protected us from harm.

The gentle warriors were taught to love their children - the youth who'd suffered the most. As we embraced compassion to guide us, we took care of the youthful version of ourselves, calming their fears in the most terrifying anxieties. We became the guardians that we had always longed for by reassuring them that we could be secure as the wars were won and the power of love and compassion are our new friends.

While we pushed forward with our mission as we walked through the wilderness, we realized that the victory of tenderness went beyond our own personal experience. The effect of our tender touching was profound. We were an example of hope for people looking for comfort within the shadows of their own personal trauma. Our stories were shared with compassion and humility knowing that for healing the power of vulnerability was unrivalled.

Dear reader, too you are a gentle warrior since you've taken on this trip with us. Every page you turn can be seen as a tribute to your courage, your determination to delve into the depths of your heart, and take in the fragments from your life.

In the midst of this chapter we should celebrate the tender wins, those achievements even if they seem insignificant, yet have immense power. Let us celebrate the spirit of warriors in us and acknowledge that our battles could be one-of-a-kind, however the strength that drives us ahead is common to all.

In those moments of calm contemplation, might you have the strength to tender to yourself, and extend the same kindness and compassion for yourself that you'd extend to a friend you love dearly. In the company of other gentle warriors, we can find comfort, encouragement, and the knowledge that we're not alone on our path.

Being a gentle warrior in the midst of the trauma of life is an empowering journey which requires determination, courage and the courage to be vulnerable. It starts with the realization that the wounds of our history are not what define us, and that deep within the depths of our suffering can be healing.

If trauma is a factor the body, it could shatter the sense of self, and make us feel lost and isolated from the world. When faced with this kind of adversity, the way for the gentle soldier begins to develop. This is a way of life which acknowledges the weight of wounds, but is unable to let them define it.

The first step to becoming gentle is cultivating self-compassion. This is the practice of showing kindness towards oneself and acknowledging that we are all human beings and worthy of compassion and love regardless of the blunders that we have done or the hurt that we've endured. Self-compassion is the lighthouse which guides us to an open acceptance of our vulnerability.

As we go through the trauma of life, we tend to construct the walls of our heart in order to shield our self from harm. But the courageous person learns that vulnerability isn't an issue, but rather an opportunity to build resilience. Through vulnerability, we are able to meet others and share our experiences, and be comforted by knowing that we're not the only ones struggling.

The role of forgiveness is crucial in the life of a gentle warrior. This isn't about accepting the acts of those who were responsible for the pain instead of getting rid of the burdens that come with carrying the burden of resentment and anger. The act of forgiveness is one of release, a chance to let go of the binds of anger and let our hearts to recover.

Through this process of transformation it is important to have the help of those around you crucial. The gentle warriors can find their strength within the companionship of fellow survivors, as well as counselors and family members who offer an open ear and without prejudice as well as in the common belief that healing can be a non-linear process.

The gentle warrior, as they take every step They learn to make the space they need for grieving, the space to experience the anger and dark moments. They develop mindfulness and learn to look at their emotions with no judgement and to take care of themselves through patience and tenderness.

In this process of accepting vulnerableness, self-compassion, as well as acceptance The gentle warrior turns their grief into motivation. They turn into advocates for changes, aiming to increase consciousness about the long-lasting effects of trauma, and the necessity of support for mental health.

In the end, being a kind warrior isn't about a specific goal rather, it's a continual determination to grow and discover yourself. It's a process that recognizes the challenges of healing through the ups and downs as well as the times of joy and victory that occur on the way.

To forgive my father was among the most difficult and transformational experiences I had as a kind soldier. As I reflected on the hurt he inflicted the forgiveness process seemed to be a mountain that was impossible to scale. The repercussions of his conduct are deep. For an extended period of time I felt the burden of resentment and anger and hurt.

In the midst of forgiveness lay the realization that clinging onto the guilt of hate kept me in prison rather than him. It was a huge amount of strength to face my feelings, admitting the harm he caused and acknowledge the fact that forgiveness is not just about blaming his actions, rather than releasing me from the shackles of hatred.

When I was trying to become an empathetic warrior, I was forced to face the armor that I had built over my heart. It was my discovery that vulnerability was not an indication of weakness but rather a way to heal. In allowing myself to be vulnerable as I grieved, to feel, and process my pain it allowed for my self-compassion to grow.

The road to forgiveness was not a straight line. There were instances that I set out on my journey and then felt backslides that made me doubt my endurance. In these times of doubt that the help of my gentle warriors as well as the advice of therapists who were compassionate was crucial.

Through therapy, I was able to reconsider my outlook and realize that forgiving was empowering- a conscious decision to become the master for my own recovery. It meant breaking away from the burdens of resentment, and not letting my past define my future.

To become a more gentle warrior, I had to the cultivation of a strong sense self-forgiveness and self-compassion. I needed to show the same compassion and empathy towards myself as I hoped to show other people. In holding myself to account for the healing I had received I had the ability to take back control in my own life.

By letting go, I realized the capacity of compassion and empathy. This helped me see my father not only as the person who caused my pain and pain, but also as a damaged and flawed individual. This did not relieve the man of any responsibility. Instead, it made him human and allowed me to let go of hate.

The road to forgiveness was marked by instances of internal conflict and emotional turmoil. This required a constant dedication to personal growth and the willingness to accept uncomfortable moments. However, in the end the victory of tenderness was an affirmation of the power of humanity's spirit, a strength which was born from the ability to forgive as well as the capacity to recover.

In the midst of trauma, a tremendous power emerges. It develops amid the broken pieces of lost innocence, and then emerges as a beacon of perseverance and faith. As you traverse the darkest parts of your personal journey I would like you to realize the fact that whatever is happening to you today is transforming your character into an extremely powerful person. Even in the face of hardship it's easy to feel defeated and shattered and to think about how this hardship could be a catalyst for resilience. Like a phoenix that rises from the grave it is possible to find strength in some of the most insignificant areas. The experiences you've had, even if they're unpleasant, are transforming your character into a gentle warrior -- a tribute to the unstoppable spirit which is within the midst of you.

It is not always easy to roar with force; often, it is quiet in moments of healing and vulnerability. It's having the courage to confront your pain head-on and to admit the hurt and confront your feelings with candor and dignity. It's persistence that allows you to persevere even when you feel like the path is impossible and the resolve to seek assistance and help in times of need.

The deepest parts of your soul is an enormous reservoir of strength - a power that can be under layers of despair and fear, but is waiting there for you to recognize it and tap into it. It's a power that comes out of the realization that you've fought the most unimaginable and, through the process of surviving, you possess the wisdom of determination.

Your path as a soft warrior could be full of challenges, turbulences and victories, but remember that, even in the midst that are unsure, your strength is never waning. The power is to forgive, accept the vulnerability of others, and extend empathy to your fellow human beings and even yourself.

Dear reader, the experience you're going through today is not what defines you, it improves your. It allows you to uncover your own determination, to uncover the beauty that lies within your wounds, and change the story of your story with a newfound power.

Be open to the change that is happening in you, as it's in the midst of suffering where the most amazing transformative events occur. Every step you make as a gracious warrior transforms you into a symbol of strength and courage and a symbol of the ability of human beings to conquer any challenge.

Chapter 5: A Heart's Journey To Wholeness"

As this gentle, and almost heroic warrior continue along the road of recovery, chapter 5 is revealed--a chapter that is awash in the radiant glow in "In the Embrace of Hope." Inside these pages, you will find an uncompromising story of love's recovery--a testimony to the unwavering path of the heart to fullness.

Even in the most bleak moments of suffering, hope may appear as a distant bright star, obscuring its brightness by the shadows of hurt. As the gentle fighter persists, hope becomes the lifeline that guides those who are struggling through the maze of healing. It's the light that calls out, "You are not defined by your past, and within you lies the strength to heal and embrace life anew."

With the hope of their hearts The gentle warrior comes to realize the power of love. The love they give to themselves as well as the affection they let others to shower on them. It is a balm which helps heal the hurts from the past while repairing the pieces that have been broken with compassion and respect.

As the traumas are etched into their skin The gentle warrior realizes that they are able to forgive. Not only those who have caused their suffering as well as themselves. This forgiveness lets the heart be free, allowing it to free itself from the burdens of anger and accept the joy that comes from the freedom of letting go.

Within the secluded zone of healing The gentle warrior is able to develop self-compassion and give it as self-care and a holy gift. They bathe their inner child with tenderness and affection accepting the vulnerability which was formerly cloaked in self-doubt. Self-compassion can be the trigger to transformation, and the key to unlock the way to completeness.

In the haze of optimism, the gentle warrior can see the beautiful side of their strength-- the amazing beauty of surviving the challenges and coming back stronger than they were the previous. The scars from injuries no longer bear the weight of shame. rather, they serve as an evidence of the strength of humankind.

With the hope of life The gentle warrior gains the confidence to dream again, and imagine a bright future full of potential, free of the past. They are able to take comfort by knowing that their past experiences do affect their life as they know that deep in the midst of their souls is the ability to build a life that is filled with joy and love.

The unending love of God extends beyond oneself and the gentle warrior extends their hand to others in their vicinity. As they heal it is an inspiration and hope to those that are on similar pathways. They are able to offer understanding, compassion and even a hand to grasp, knowing that the path to healing will be better when sharing it with others.

It is my wish to let you know that the love of God will be waiting for you, too. The gentleness of healing is the possibility of love's redemption - a loving relationship that will take through the most difficult times and carry you up to new levels of strength.

Be grateful for the gift of self-compassion and forgiveness as they can be the key for unlocking the doors to your soul and setting you free. Remember that your scars aren't a sign of vulnerability, but rather a testament to your resilience, the ability to persevere, be healed, and flourish.

With the radiant warmth of the hope that surrounds you, be able to experience the ability of love to repair your broken soul as well as the strength to reinvent your dreams. You're a kind warrior, a fighter, an example of courage and a testimony to humanity's unshakeable spirit.

The hopefulness of a friend is one that is able to walk hand-in-hand with the gentle warrior as they embark on the path of healing trauma. It's a power that gives life to the most dark corners of your heart and aids in navigating the path toward wholeness and strength.

In the beginning of healing trauma may engulf the patient in darkness that obscures any glimpse of optimism. However, in the midst of our hurt, hope is revealed as a shining ray of hope, a light that says, "You can heal, and you are not defined by your past."

It isn't about denial of the fact that we are suffering instead, it is about accepting that there is an opportunity for transformation, and that the future could differ from the previous. The enduring conviction that healing isn't impossible, but it is possible.

The gentle warrior is embraced by optimism, they find the strength to confront the trauma with a wide heart. Hope is a shield that protects against the darkness of despair by reminding the heart there's hope regardless of how difficult the path isn't easy.

With hopefulness, the gentle warrior sets goals for their journey towards healing. They dream of a life that is free of the chains of traumatic experiences, full of joy, love and purpose. Hope can be the star which helps them overcome obstacles and setbacks with the knowledge that every step will lead them closer to the vision of a complete life.

Self-compassion is the gentle voice which reassures the heart wounded that it's fine to fall and stumble. It inspires gentle warriors to show the same compassion towards themselves as they would give to a beloved friend. If you are feeling vulnerable

Hopefulness lends a gentle helping hand and inspires the person to continue.

One of the greatest advantages of a positive outlook is the ability to bring together peaceful warriors within a circle of strength. When survivors gather and find comfort in being aware that they're not the only ones struggling. Sharing their hopes can be a source of strength. The community of support creates a tapestry of strength.

When the journey of healing is unfolding, optimism fills the process with meaning and purpose. Every day is an opportunity to live each day with hope and cherish the times of growth and improvement. A sense of optimism allows the gentle warrior to be grateful for even the most modest victories, knowing that these are steps in the direction of healing.

When you are in doubt Hopefulness is an unshakeable partner that reminds the gentle soldier of the change which has already occurred. It helps them take a look back at the journey they've taken and is a testimony to the strength of hope and perseverance.

Accept hope by having an open and loving heart. Let it light your path as you traverse the challenges of healing after trauma. With the hopefulness of your surroundings it will give you the confidence to face your suffering, the determination to stand up, and confidence that healing is in your reach.

Be hopeful Be hopeful, no matter how the journey appears long and difficult. This is the friend who can help you get through the toughest times and help you live an existence of completeness and happiness. Take advantage of the strength of hope. In its luminous luminescence, you'll see the strength and beauty of the aftermath of the trauma.

One of the best source of optimism is realizing that you're not on your own in this adventure. Many others have traveled or are walking along the exact path you see you walking. In this experience of sharing that seed of hope is planted and grow.

A gentle warrior might be feeling isolated and believe that their pain is only theirs to carry. However, within the huge web of humanity There are many threads interspersed with tales of strength, resilience and healing. Every thread is a story of a person affected by trauma and in each of them, there is always hope.

Being hopeful in the life of others is an amazing signpost to the power of humanity's spirit. It's a reminder that despite the hurt of fear, pain, and the dark There are people who have walked through similar challenges, and came out better for this experience. The bonds of kinship can provide comfort, being aware that you're not the only one struggling.

Within the hugs of a the community, gentle warriors can find the support and understanding they need. Sharing empathy is a vital thread that connects hearts, spanning the distance of time and space. When you meet people suffering from an emotional trauma, it becomes apparent that you're an integral part of a tapestry which demonstrates the strength of humanity.

Through sharing experiences, gentle warriors are able to learn from each other. They learn strategies, insights and strategies for coping that they can apply to their own journey to healing. Being able to observe the development and improvement of others can give hope -- a glimpse of possibilities to them.

When the gentle warrior is able to open their hearts to the tales of their fellow soldiers and begins to observe the reflections of their own experience within their fellows. This reflection of shared struggle and triumph can be an incredibly powerful proof of humanity's universal life. It demonstrates that we're not all alone when we face challenges as a group, and that as a group, we can lift and encourage our fellow human beings.

Through this network of healing, hope is given an empowering collective force. The hope of each person becomes an inspiration for other people, and their optimism becomes an engine that helps the community move ahead.

Dear reader, as you embark on your healing journey, be aware that you're a part of a huge community of warriors, survivors and those who have been through it all. Your journey is distinct and shared. Your bravery to deal with your experience can inspire and encourage others. Rely on the strength of your community, and take comfort in the experience of others who have been on the same route you're on.

Through sharing stories, shared experiences and encouragement You will discover hope all around you. Take advantage of this common wellspring of optimism, as it will help you navigate through the most difficult times and remind you that there is no need to be alone. We are all on the same way to healing and through the unification of our faith and faith, we create a new possible future that is resilient and hopeful.

Invigorating your faith reserves can be an empowering experience in the search for communities that are composed of gentle men and women who share an aim: to get out of the crushing hold of trauma, and to find tranquility in the midst of turmoil. They are places of compassion, understanding and support. Hope thrives because of the power of sharing experiences.

With the companionship of gentle warriors, you experience the deep sense of community--a feeling of belonging that goes beyond language and expresses the hidden truths of the soul. You aren't considered a victim or a misunderstood person and are instead embraced by hearts and arms. Within this circle of souls who understand where the seed of hope is planted and grows.

The stories of perseverance and triumph that pervade these communities can be the source of optimism. While you relate your experience and learn that you're not the only one in the struggles you face, but also, you are not alone in your victories. Every story of healing fuels the confidence of those around you and triggers a chain reaction that inspires and empowers.

In these societies, the notion of hope isn't just a idea but an actual power that pushes you to greater heights even in facing of challenges. It's the affirming the presence of other travelers who are on the road to fullness who are there to hold your hand during the darkest hours and celebrating your triumphs, regardless of the size.

The transformation that others undergo can fill your heart with hope. The tales of brave warriors who overcome the darkness of pain to find comfort and recovery are beacons of light that illuminate how to proceed. It becomes clear the possibility of healing yourself. not merely a chance, rather, it is a possibility you declare to be yours.

Communities become wellsprings of optimism, nourishing your soul with support and acceptance. While you give your help to those around you, you recognize that you have the ability to motivate and inspire others through your own personal journey. Collectively, you are an entire force. A force which refuses to be determined by past events and instead, sets off on a path to healing and strength.

Within the sacred spaces of the gentle warrior community the hope of overcoming obstacles becomes a collective song that unites the voices of those who have suffered and resonates throughout the hearts of everyone. Hope's chorus fuels the determination of your heart to remind the you that you're not only a spectator of your own life. You are actively involved in the healing process.

When you dive deeper into these groups there is an inherent sense of purpose that is over and above your personal health. You are a source confidence for those around you, extending the assistance of people who are having difficulty navigating their own path. In giving hope, the act is a powerful elixir that boosts your personal reserves, and feeds the entire spirit.

Be grateful for the possibility of joining community of gentle warriors just like yourself, as they're an inspiration that will breathe life to your healing journey. Begin by surrounded by people who can understand, encourage and inspire you. Find inspiration in the stories of perseverance and let the power of the community of faith fuel your determination to tackle the obstacles in the future.

Within those communities, the light of optimism will shine stronger than ever, sweeping off the fears and doubts. As a uniting strength of faith, you'll not only be able to find tranquility within yourself, but generate a wave of healing that goes far beyond your personal experience.

At the end of this book, my dear readers I offer you a message of hope which will lift your spirit and lead to the dazzling perspective of a new day.

As you embrace the hope You aren't alone. You're surrounded by a group of gentle warriors who are there with you and offer comfort in understanding, compassion, and confidence. Through this kinship of sacred trust that you're a part of, you're noticed appreciated, heard and appreciated by the determination which propels your forward.

While you travel the road of healing, be aware that your hope is not just only a fleeting glimpse, instead, it's a burning fire that burns in your heart. It's the confidence that you are able to conquer adversity as well as the capability to come out of the deepest darkness and embrace the dawn of the new day.

Within the rich tapestry of shared memories, you can find peace the knowledge that your journey is interwoven with many others, a testimony to humanity's spirit's power to heal and change. Your path is not an experience of solitude and isolation, but one of interconnectedness that is, where your faith will inspire hope for others and in turn, you create an octet of victory.

Be a part of the community, the communal heartbeat that feeds the hope you have and boosts your determination. By bringing hope to other people, you replenish the wellspring of your own, as optimism is unlimited and generous in the life of gentle warriors.

While you travel ahead, keep in mind that hope isn't just an abstract concept it is a power which is within you, the power that ignites desires, drives determination and enables you to alter the story of your life. You are equipped to recover, the wisdom to accept forgiveness and to accept the moment and embrace the present with the open arms of a child.

With the warm arms of optimism and love, you realize that this triumph isn't just a dream but rather a birthright, a birthright which belongs to you dear reader. Each time you step out in the direction of a soft warrior believe that you're creating an era of resilience happiness, joy, and limitless possibilities.

In the final moments of this chapter, let the hope-filled sigh remain in your soul. It will guide you on the path of light ahead. Your identity is not determined by your history, but rather by your ability to overcome every day - the strength that turns suffering into triumph and scars into wisdom.

Be awestruck by hope as your faithful partner, as it'll accompany you in the dark and encircle you through the sun's rays. In its radiance it will give you the strength to find your soul, revise your own story then emerge as a graceful fighter, a symbol of hope, perseverance, and the eternal determination of love's eternal forgiveness.

Do you travel this road in the confidence that you're not on your own Your journey is surrounded by a vast world of possibility and hope. You're a gentle soldier, a source of optimism as a testimony to the unstoppable human spirit. Take hold of the hope that is promised to you and it will forever help you find the peace of totality.

When you are on your way toward wholeness, may the faith in love's eternal redemption open the way for a new life full of joy, healing and endless possibilities. With the help of faith and faith, you will find that redemption you've always wanted as well as the beauty that emerges out of the rubble of trauma. It is not your fault, and you're stronger than you think. Accept the promises of hope and it will lead you into the light of a heart that is whole.

Chapter 6: Tears That Changed Us

"Sculpting Resilience: The Art of Embracing Vulnerability"

In the tranquil space in chapter 6, we enter into the sanctuaries of "Tears That Molded Us," where the core of resilience is created by the act of accepting vulnerability. In the echoes of our common experiences and experiences, we can find peace by understanding that tears aren't only an expression of grief, they also serve as a testimony to the power of human spirit.

Like sparkling pearls, create the fabric of our healing journey, with each one is a reflection of our emotions emanating from the deepest part of our hearts. In the acknowledgement of our vulnerability that we are able to realize the transformational effect of tears - their power to heal, cleanse and transform us into more resilient creatures.

After a trauma the vulnerability can be viewed as a flaw in armor, a flaw to hide. But, as warriors who are gentle are taught that vulnerability isn't something to be avoided, but instead it is a source of immense force. In the sluggish place of vulnerability where we can find the strength to accept our suffering and to accept our feelings and recover from those hurts that were once threatening to devour us.

When we cry, we shed the burdens we've endured for so long: the weight of words that have not been spoken as well as the ache from not letting go of tears, and the remnants of hurts from our past. Each tear transforms into a sacred offer, an affirmation of our capacity to deeply feel, recognize our suffering and to take back emotions as tools for healing.

When we accept our vulnerability, we are able to experience the power of connecting--the capacity to build real bonds with those who are on the same journey. In the sharing of vulnerability that we meet friends who can understand each other without any words, who support us with no judgement and walk alongside us on the path of healing.

Accepting your vulnerability does not mean residing in despair, but rather realizing that vulnerability can be the first step towards resilient. Through vulnerability, you can tap into the reservoir of our strength, the strength to be resilient, to let go, and to build our lives again with a fresh sense of purpose.

Be grateful for your tears, as a testimony of your strength and capability to be healed. Every tear you shed is an expression of your strength, a work of art by the depths of vulnerability.

Be open to the vulnerability within you. It will lead to transformation. When you are in a state of emotional turmoil Do not be afraid of the feelings that come up instead let them run like a river to cleanse and replenish your soul. In the stream of tears that we experience an outlet, like a raindrop that provides freshness to the drained surface of our souls.

While you are on your process of healing, keep in mind that your tears aren't an indication of weakness, instead, they're a sign of the humanity of you. Be open to vulnerability as a source of strength which allows you to bond with other people in a way that allows you to share and accept kindness, and also to see your beauty in the raw realness of your feelings.

The tears that formed us, we learn the essence of resilience--the ability to accept vulnerability, permitting it to transform us into warriors with compassion and strength. Every tear is a stroke that creates the art of recovery, which is a symbol of the strength which emerges from the depths of hurt.

It isn't weakness, it's an incredibly powerful strength that is able to ignite the flames of resilience in ourselves. Being gentle warriors, we take vulnerability as a sacred blessing because it is the door to our true self and opens the door to growth that is transformational.

In a society that is awash in stoicism and emotional armor the vulnerability of our souls is an act of bravery and a testimony to the willingness of us to show up as real and authentic. It requires a lot of courage to remove the layers which protect our souls as we expose our feelings, and be vulnerable in sharing our experiences with complete and honest.

By being vulnerable, we can are able to connect with our feelings, and allow ourselves to be vulnerable and feel our feelings without fear of judgement. This is the way to be vulnerable and face our most intimate realities that we find our strength, the unwavering ability to overcome adversity with grace and determination.

If we accept vulnerability, we are opening us to the possibility of healing. In vulnerability lets go of the burdens of traumas from the past, allowing the pain-filled tears to be cleansed and nourish the soul's soil to allow new seeds of optimism and strength will take root.

When we are vulnerable, we can find the strength within our flaws and the scars we've incurred. We realize that the scars we have are not what define us, instead, they serve as an evidence of our resilience, the tangible evidence of our strength and our determination to triumph over our worst moment.

By being vulnerable, we tear up the barriers that keep us from each other. Through the vulnerability of our fellow humans that we discover connection and understanding, forming bridges that cross the distances between us. The vulnerability of our lives is the glue which binds us all and weaves together a web of common hope.

Let's dispel the idea that vulnerability is the sign of weakness. Instead, let us embrace vulnerability as a fundamental aspect of who we are, the fuel which propels us to development and healing. It is a feat of courage to accept our feelings as well as to be able to be acknowledged, and then embrace the vulnerability of discovery of oneself.

Being gentle warriors, we take vulnerability seriously, not as something to hide rather as the stone of our resiliency--a lighthouse that teaches us acceptance, self-compassion and improvement. We should cultivate vulnerability to create a space for change, in which the blossoms of healing blossom in dazzling colors.

Through the soft embrace of our vulnerability we gain the strength to confront our fears, ask for help when it is needed and be able to acknowledge the complexity of our emotions. Through vulnerability, can we gain the ability to create our own stories--a story of hope, strength and self-compassion.

When we go through the healing process, keep in mind that vulnerability isn't weak; it's an incredibly potent potion that feeds our spirit and propels us to fullness. Be vulnerable with kindness and compassion, as it can lead you towards the purest embodiment of who you are.

Within the vulnerability, there are resilient seeds. They are the ones that when watered with self-acceptance and compassion blossom into beautiful blossoms of faith. Accept your vulnerability dear reader, as in its soft embrace is your path to accepting your full strength and your beautiful humanness.

It's not all about wearing a shield that is impervious to attack or hiding our feelings. True strength is in the acceptance of vulnerability - the ability to open up, be honest and genuine regarding our feelings, experiences as well as struggles. The courage is to cut through the protective layers and to let ourselves see ourselves in all our rawness as well as our flaws.

It's not about denial or burying our hurt, rather, facing the pain with a strong heart. It's in the midst of our vulnerability where we discover the strength to confront the hurts we have suffered, cry tears of healing and release our burdens. Through vulnerability, can we discover the sources of strength within us.

By accepting our vulnerability, we acknowledge our vulnerability and it's complexities. It is acceptable to be vulnerable, to be unsure, and to ask for help when we need it. Our true strength lies in our desire to reach out for a connection with people and build bridges to understand. It's the ability to get up again after each accident, to emerge from the rubble of our hurt, and continue going forward in unrelenting determination.

The definition of strength is not just a strong appearance, but rather an embracing acceptance of our feelings. It's the courage to accept being vulnerable even when it is uncomfortable or scary. In the process of being vulnerable, we discover that tears aren't evidence of weakness, rather, they're the release of feelings that have been held back.

Being gentle warriors, we demonstrate true strength in navigating our journey of healing using the vulnerability of our guide. We develop self-compassion, and then offer it to others knowing that we're all walking our own paths, each with their own traumas and stories. The real strength is in creating each other's space by offering help, as well as sharing stories of courage and sincerity.

The truth is that strength can't be located in a lack of vulnerability but instead in it's celebration. It's about being aware of our suffering and accepting our resilience, a delicate equilibrium which lets us improve and heal. True strength comes from the practice of accepting vulnerability, carving the resilience of tears and shaping our lives through love and optimism.

Be aware that the true strength is within you. It is the strength that allows you to feel vulnerable, be vulnerable, to feel deeply and overcome your past traumas. Accept vulnerability as a tool to help you and it will be an essential ingredient to open the way to resilience and the way to embrace your full strength - the ability to transform your character into a soft fighter of compassion, courage and unwavering faith.

Accept your vulnerability by embracing it with a heart that is open, dear reader. Let your tears speak to the splendor of your resilient. With the soft hug of vulnerability lies the creation of your strength--a piece of work created through tears that were shaped by love and drenched in optimism. You're a piece of art, a testimony to the strength of humankind and the strength of accepting the vulnerability in a way that is graceful and strong.

To my courageous and resilient reader,

While I am with you on the healing process and journey, I'd like to take the time to recognize your unwavering power and extraordinary endurance. It hasn't been easy because it's adorned by the marks of traumas from your past and the weight of difficult feelings. However, throughout it all you've embraced your the vulnerability of your situation, turning your pain into victory and tears into hope.

You're a peaceful soldier, and your path can be seen as a tribute to humanity's indomitable spirit. Every step you make regardless of how tiny you may think it to be, is a tremendous action of bravery that brings you towards the bright perspective of healing and completeness. You should be aware that every step you take however small can be, should inspire celebration.

If you're in uncertainty, keep in mind that healing does not happen in a linear fashion every day is a new opportunity for fresh opportunities to grow and change. It is not a sign of weakness but rather an expression of your courage to face the pain you are experiencing by embracing it with a heart that is open. Accept them as they're the purifying rain which nurtures the hope seeds inside your.

While you explore the path of healing, be aware that you're not the only one. In the experiences shared by other gentle warriors You will be able to find comfort and compassion. A community of support who is there for you and offers a hand to grasp and a shoulder to support.

Your experience is personal and precious, and it is by letting yourself be vulnerable to discover the strength which is within the person you are. Let your emotions flow in their ebb and flow because they're the hues that create your canvas for therapeutic journey. It's a piece of art created by the deepest part of your own authenticity.

Even in the darkest of times there's a glimmer of optimism that burns inside your soul. It is a flame that will not be snuffed out. Be sure to nurture that flame because it's a beacon which will guide you out of the darkness and to the sway of peace.

Chapter 7: Whispers Of Solace

"Embracing Brokenness: Finding Sanctuary in Each Other"

Within the welcoming refuge in Chapter 7 we are taken upon a path of deep bonding-- a voyage of "Whispers of Solace" where vulnerability becomes the source of healing, and the sanctuary of our lives can be found in the loving hug of each other. In this chapter, in the tender movement that is vulnerability, we are able to see the strength of human connections--the threads that unite us through shared memories of trauma from childhood.

The vast expanse of brokenness, we can find peace in knowing we're not all alone. Every heart is carrying the burden of their own wounds. In our shared pain it is possible to see humanity's resilience as beautiful, and the ability to heal the broken pieces of our souls, and to restore our lives to a new motivation.

In the quiet of our souls and comfort, we are able to tell our tales--the unsaid thoughts that have persisted in our souls. Through sharing the stories, we weave a web of mutual understanding, weaving in threads of compassion and empathy that connect us. It's in the sanctuary of vulnerability that healing can take roots.

By accepting our brokenness in accepting our brokenness, we realize that life is not an untouched canvas but rather a collection of broken pieces, which holds in them the capacity to make something wonderful. Every broken piece transforms into a brushstroke within the masterpiece of our resiliency--a work of art that is painted using the joy of laughter, tears along with the fine art of surviving.

Being gentle warriors, we hold the space of one another while we traverse the maze of healing. With the gentle whispers of comfort we do not make judgements or solutions instead, we offer a secure refuge in which our weaknesses are addressed by kindness and compassion. Through this safe haven of acceptance there is the strength to heal, and the strength to go on.

Solace's whispers are transformed into a song of love and connection, a tune that transcends the limits of space and time connecting peaceful warriors throughout the vastness of human existence. In the act of listening that we give our presence as a cure for wounds that words can't heal.

With the gentle whispers of relief We discover the power of sharing compassion. If we offer a helping arm to lift someone else up in return, we feel being lifted up as well. Through the simple act of being supportive of one another and letting others help us, we discover the endless capacity of strength inside our own.

Dear reader, within the midst the pages of this book, I'd like you to understand that you don't define yourself through your flaws instead, by the strength that comes from within. Because it is through the vulnerability of your fellow human beings that you are able to find safety within one another, a place in which healing can be nurtured and hope can be reborn.

When you are on the path to healing, be aware that your flaws are not an issue, but rather a testimony to the strength you have. When we embrace our brokenness, it is that we gain the capacity to change our narratives, turning the pain into meaning, wounds to wisdom, and blemishes become symbols of our survival.

As you listen to the whispers of peace In the hushed whispers of solace, feel secure the knowledge that you're never by yourself. As a group, we create an enlightened community and each of us is a testimony to the beautiful that emerges out of the depths of hurt. Take a step forward in this shared journey because within it is the source of healing, that heart beating with the heartbeat of compassion and the harmony of the hope.

Find comfort by being embraced by each other, and let the whispers of peace become the soothing lullaby that guides your heart through the dark days of recovery. There is no need to be in a lonely place, dear reader. In the soothing whispers you're surrounded by an army of peaceful warriors that are united in affection, love and the undying optimism.

While we go on our adventure together Let the gentle whispers of comfort lead you. Let connections create a tapestry of strength which spans the space and time. Be grateful for your imperfections as an affirmation of your resilience and let the space of mutual compassion become your sanctuary in which healing will take off.

While we traverse the path that is "Whispers of Solace," we dig deeper into the deep realities that arise from the sanctum of mutual compassion. When we are embraced by our fellow human beings, we discover an inner strength that allows us to walk through the path of healing, the one that takes us to the core of our the self and resilience.

Through the sighs of calm We learn that vulnerability isn't an indicator of weakness rather a sign of the humanity of us. It's the way into connection, an open bridge that stretches across the gulf between isolation and welcomes us into the comfort of heartfelt hearts.

Being gentle warriors, we discover that by sharing our struggles, we don't just find healing for ourselves and our loved ones, but also provide faith for those around us. Being vulnerable is an invitation to others to accept their own authenticity, to share their own stories and take comfort in knowing that they're not the only ones.

In the sanctum of shared vulnerability, we break down the cloaks of shame which may have held us back in a long time. It is clear that the experiences, tears and scars not reasons for hiding and are instead badges of strength that show the strength of our strength.

With the sound of solace through the whispers of solace, we are mirrors reflecting the power and beauty of the warriors around us. Every story we share is a woven tapestry of hope and a testimony to our human capacity to conquer adversity, and to regain our strength.

In the current chapter in the book "Whispers of Solace," we learn to embrace the strength of compassion, a soft touch that eases our pain and allows us the opportunity to offer the same compassion to those around us. In allowing space for our fellow human beings' vulnerabilities We discover that our hearts grow, and become vessels for love and compassion.

I'd like to remind you that the journey you've taken is important. Your triumphs, your pain and your strength--all of it counts. Your identity is not determined by your history, but rather by the determination you have every single day to conquer it.

In the midst of mutual compassion, we can see the profound human bond--the reality that we're united by shared experience of joy as well as sorrow as well as triumph and struggle. In extending kindness to one another it is clear that the pain we feel isn't an isolated burden, but rather it is a bridge that connects people together.

If you are embracing your woundedness, be aware that you're also acknowledging your ability to heal. Cracks that you feel in your heart aren't a sign of vulnerability, but rather openings for the hope of healing to penetrate. Accept your life story because it's the story that has made you the courageous and resilient spirit that you are now.

With the gentle whispers of comfort take peace knowing that you're surrounded by a family of caring hearts. A community that recognizes the strength of your character, beauty and worth. Every step taken to heal is a testimony to the courage you display and the incredible power of humankind.

In the final pages of this chapter take a moment to let the gentle whispers of peace be a part of your soul and a gentle reminder there is no one else when you travel this path. The pain you feel isn't an unassailable burden and is a sacred bond which binds us in the form of gentle warriors.

The sanctuary of compassion for all be an oasis where healing can flourish as gentle whispers of hope help you navigate through the darkness and illuminate the way to the future that is filled with optimism and resilience. And an unwavering embrace from each others.

Take heed to the soothing whispers to you dear reader for in their soft cadence is the assurance that you're not on your own. We, in a collective force for healing, we'll keep trying to light the way ahead, one step at an time, one sound every now and then, until we arrive at the radiant final destination of unconditional love's eternal salvation.

There is no need to be in a lonely place, dear reader. and within the quiet whispers of peace, you'll always be able to find a safe-haven within each other. Take advantage of the bonds that connect us all, because it's within this connection where we experience the joy of healing as well as the capacity of human beings to persevere, be healed, and ultimately to flourish.

I'd like to reassure your with absolute certainty that you aren't alone. With the words shared by these people You are in the midst of the hearts of a loving community that are with you throughout the path to healing.

Within the vast field of pain, keep in mind that you're not alone in the maze of healing. Many gentle warriors have traversed the same path as you and each has left the path of strength and endurance. They are aware of the torrent of tears as well as the challenges you confront because they've been through the same challenges.

In the hushed whispers of comfort Find comfort knowing that you're being heard and acknowledged. Your life story is important as do your personal experiences. appreciated. It is not just a single tourist; you're part of a tapestry made of people who share experiences as well as souls.

If you ever feel overwhelmed by the burden from your life, be aware that there are soft hearts waiting to help you. Take a step forward, and there will be hands ready to support you. The vulnerability of you is accepted with kindness as well as your feelings are treated with love.

In the refuge of our sharing compassion, we remain in solidarity, offering comfort for one another. While we care for the brokenness of one another with tenderness as we learn the reality that we're united by the human condition: fragile but resilient, hurt and healed, but forever linked.

The sighs of comfort do not just appear as pages of words and they're a powerful truth that resonates in the souls of gentle men. There is no need to be alone my dear reader. You are loved, respected and respected for your courage when you face your journey to healing.

In the midst of all the dark clouds that occasionally obscure your way be assured that there's an enveloping chorus of love and love that surrounds you. We celebrate your victories and rejoice with you; and in the midst of your challenges, we provide an unshakeable help. You're part of the community of people who hold them in their heart regardless of the most difficult of times.

When doubt and worry knock the doors of your soul, recollect the hints of hope which ring within you. You don't have to be isolated. Be vulnerable, and allow it to be your beacon to draw people closer. With the comfort of a the bonds of friendship, you'll discover strength and healing.

I'd like to assure you that you are loved by everyone Your story is weaved into the experiences we share. Within the sway the swaying of "Whispers of Solace," you'll find a refuge--an place where you can be met by acceptance, compassion and endless gratitude.

There is no need to be alone and inside the comforting echoes of your soul it is possible to find an oasis, a place to rest in one the other. Take advantage of the bonds that connect our hearts, as it's within this connection where we experience the wonder of healing as well as the capacity of human beings to persevere, recover, and thrive. Your contribution is cherished of the journey and you'll never travel by yourself.

In the tranquil sanctuary in chapter 6, we are welcomed into the sacred space "Tears That Molded Us," where the core of resilience is revealed through the act of accepting vulnerability. There, in the echoes of shared memories We find comfort by understanding that tears aren't just an expression of sorrow, but are also an expression of the power of human spirit.

The tears, like sparkling pearls, create the elaborate tapestry that is the healing process. Each one is represents the emotion emanating from the depths that our inner souls. When we are able to accept the vulnerability of our vulnerability that we are able to realize the transformational potential of tears, their ability to heal, cleanse and transform us into more resilient creatures.

After a trauma it is easy to see vulnerability as a flaw in armor -- a weakness that needs to be hidden. However, as gentle warriors are taught that vulnerability isn't an obstacle, but rather it is a source of immense force. It is within the slender area of vulnerability that we can find the strength to accept our suffering and to accept our feelings and recover from the scars that used to threaten to consume us.

When we cry, we shed the burdens that we've been carrying for so long - the burden of words that have not been spoken and the pain of unshed tears, and the lingering effects of hurts from the past. Every tear can be a holy offer, an affirmation of our ability to deeply feel, admit our hurt and to take back our feelings as tools for healing.

When we accept our vulnerability, we are able to experience connections are a powerful force, allowing us to build genuine bonds with people who are on the same journey. In the shared vulnerability that we can find like-minded people, those who are able to understand with no the use of words, who embrace our hand without judgement, and walk alongside us on the path of healing.

The art of accepting vulnerability doesn't mean dwelling in desperation, but accepting that vulnerability is the first step towards the ability to overcome. In vulnerability you can tap into the reservoir of our strength, the strength to endure, let go, and restore our lives to a new sense of purpose.

Be grateful for your tears, as a testimony to your strength and ability to be healed. Every tear that you shed represents an expression of your strength and resilience, an art work created by the depths of vulnerability.

Be open to the vulnerability in you because it will lead to transformation. When you are in a state of emotional turmoil don't shy away from your emotions instead let them run like a river to cleanse and replenish your soul. When we let go of tears that we experience an outlet, like a raindrop that provides freshness to the depleted surface of our souls.

While you are on your path of healing, be aware that your tears aren't an indicator of weakness they are a testimony to your humanness. Accept your vulnerability as a blessing which allows you to be a bridge between people as well as to give and receive empathy, and discover your beauty in the raw realness of your feelings.

Through the shattered tears that formed us, we can discover the essence of resilience-- the practice of accepting vulnerability and let it shape our character into warriors of compassion and strength. Each tear turns into a line on the canvas of our healing, a testimony to the splendor which emerges from the depths of suffering.

It isn't weakness, it's an incredibly powerful strength that sparks the flames of resilience in our beings. We, as gentle warriors accept vulnerability as an opulent gift because it is the way to reveal our real self and opens the door to transformative change.

In a culture that favors stoicism, emotional protection being vulnerable is seen as an act of bravery and a testimony to our ability to stand out as real and authentic. It requires a lot of courage to remove the layers which protect our souls as we expose the emotions that we carry, and be vulnerable in sharing our experiences with complete and honest.

By being vulnerable, we can are able to connect with our feelings, and allow ourselves to experience our emotions without restriction or judgement. In this willingness to be vulnerable and face our most intimate realities that we find our strength, the unwavering ability to confront adversity gracefully and determination.

In embracing vulnerability, we are opening us to the possibility of healing. In vulnerability lets go of the burdens of traumas from the past, allowing the pain of tears to be cleansed and replenish the soul's soil to allow new seeds of resilience and hope will take root.

When we are vulnerable, we can find resilience in the imperfections of our lives as well as our scars. Our scars are not what define us; rather, they are an evidence of our resilience, the tangible evidence of our strength and our determination to overcome our most difficult times.

By being vulnerable, we tear up the barriers that keep us from each other. In our vulnerability together that we discover connection and compassion, building bridges of understanding that cross the chasms between us. The vulnerability of our lives is the glue which binds us all and weaves a web of hope shared by all.

Let's dispel the idea that vulnerability is an indication of weakness. Instead, we should celebrate it as a part of our being, and the energy that drives us toward improvement and healing. It requires a lot of strength to accept our feelings as well as to be able to be acknowledged, and then be vulnerable to the process of self-discovery.

Being gentle warriors, we accept vulnerability, not as something that needs to be concealed rather as the mainstay of our resilience, a lighthouse that teaches us compassion, understanding, and improvement. We should cultivate vulnerability as an oasis of growth and healing, where the blooms of healing blossom with vibrant colors.

Through the soft embrace of our vulnerability we discover the strength to confront the fears that we have, seek assistance when we need it and be able to acknowledge the complexities of our feelings. Through vulnerability, can we gain the ability to craft our own personal narratives, a one of courage, optimism and self-love.

While we traverse the stages of healing keep in mind that vulnerability does not mean weak; it's an incredibly potent potion that feeds our souls and pushes our bodies towards completeness. Accept your vulnerability with compassion and compassion, as it will lead you towards the purest manifestation of you.

Within the vulnerability are the roots of resilience. These are the seeds that when nurtured by self-acceptance and compassion, blossom into beautiful blooms of optimism. Accept your vulnerability dear reader, as it is within its warm embrace the way to embrace the wholeness of your power and your beautiful humanness.

It's not the result of wearing an armor that is impenetrable or hiding our feelings. True strength is in the acceptance of vulnerability

- the ability to open up, be honest and genuine about our experiences, emotions and challenges. It's the ability to cut through the veil of security and let ourselves see ourselves in all our vulnerability and flaws.

The definition of strength isn't about denigrating or concealing pain rather, facing the pain with courage. In the vulnerability of our souls where we discover the ability to recognize our own wounds as well as cry tears of healing and release the burdens that we bear. Through vulnerability, can we discover the sources of strength within us.

By accepting our vulnerability, we acknowledge our vulnerability and its complexities. We acknowledge that it's acceptable to be vulnerable, to fall, and get help when it is needed. Our true strength lies in our determination to reach out to reach out and connect with other people, and to create bridges of mutual understanding. It's the ability to rise up from every stumble, to rise again from the dust of suffering, and keep going forward in unshakeable determination.

The definition of strength is not just a strong appearance, but an embracing hug to our emotions. It's the ability to accept being vulnerable even when it is uncomfortable or scary. In the process of being vulnerable, we discover that we aren't evidence of weakness, they are the expression of emotions that were for a long time kept in a cage.

We, as gentle warriors are truly strong in navigating the healing process using our vulnerableness as our guide. We develop self-compassion, and then offer it to others knowing that we're all walking our own paths, each with their own injuries and experience. The real strength is in creating each other's space providing support and sharing stories of courage and honesty.

In the end, strength cannot be located in the lack of vulnerability instead, it is in the celebration of vulnerability. It's about accepting our vulnerability and acknowledging our resilience, a delicate equilibrium which lets us improve and heal. True strength lies in the practice of embracing vulnerability, carving the resilience of tears and shaping our lives by embracing hope and love.

Keep in mind that your true strength lies in you, the ability to let yourself be vulnerable, be vulnerable, to feel deeply and transcend your struggles. Be open to vulnerability as an ally and it will be crucial to unlock the way to resilience and the way to embrace the wholeness of your power--the force that transforms you into a graceful soldier of strength, love and unwavering hope.

Be vulnerable with a wide heart dear reader as you let the tears serve as an affirmation of the power of your strength. With the soft acceptance of vulnerability is the shaping of your resilience, a piece of work created through tears and love and drenched in faith. Your life is a work of art, a testimony to humanity's indomitable spirit as well as the strength of accepting the vulnerability in a way that is graceful and strong.

To my courageous and resilient reader,

While I am with you on the healing process I would like to take the time to acknowledge your unwavering strength and incredible determination. The path you have taken hasn't been easy because it's adorned by the marks left by past traumas as well as the burden of adversity emotional states. However, throughout it all you've accepted your vulnerableness, and transformed your pain into victory and tears to possibility.

You're a graceful fighter, and your experience can be seen as a tribute to the unstoppable human spirit. Every step regardless of how tiny it is an action of bravery that brings you to the dazzling new horizon of wholeness and healing. You should realize that the progress you make however small can be a reason for celebration.

If you're in a moment of anxiety, be reminded that healing does not happen in a linear fashion Every day offers fresh opportunities to grow and change. The tears you shed aren't a sign of weakness, they are an expression of your courage to face the pain you are experiencing and with a caring heart. Accept them as they're the wash that nurtures the seeds faith inside the person you.

When you travel through the terrain of healing, remember that you're not on your own. Through the shared stories of your fellow warriors of gentle nature and healers, you can find peace and compassion. A community of support who is there for you with a helping hand take and a heart to pull on.

Your experience is personal as well as sacred. It is by letting yourself be vulnerable in which you discover the power which is within your. Let your emotions flow in their ebb and flow as they're your colors on the picture of your recovery journey, a work of art crafted by the depths of the authenticity you possess.

In the midst of the most difficult times there's a glimmer of optimism that burns inside your soul. It is a flame that will not be snuffed out. Be sure to nurture that flame because it's a beacon of light which will guide you out of the darkness and towards the peace of.

Dear reader, the strength you have cannot be measured by the traumatic experiences you've endured or endured, but rather by how you overcome the challenges. Your healing journey is a celebration of the magnificence of human spirit - the ability to thrive in the face of adversity, find optimism in the midst of despair and embrace the vulnerability that is a source of resilience.

Keep honoring the healing process and know that it's not a goal, but an ongoing sacred process. Take care of yourself and your journey, appreciate the progress you have made as well as remember that this journey will be a testimony to your strength.

While you go through the phases that are healing for you, I would like you to cling to this fact: you're deserving of compassion, love and happiness. It may be a long and difficult road and difficult, but you're more resilient. In you lies the ability to heal, transform and embrace all that life has to offer.

Chapter 8: Talking About The Childhood Trauma

The chapter will discuss the significance of speaking the door to childhood trauma. Learn the importance of confronting the fears you have, accepting your vulnerability and self-compassion in the beginning steps towards recovering.

Within the tiniest recesses of our minds is a hidden world. A space filled with memories emotions and memories of our past which could be buried in our own. These are the remains of the traumas that we experienced as children, memories of events that created lasting scars for our hearts. Women have to carry these burdens without realizing their impact in our souls. This

The chapter will examine the significance of speaking out about childhood trauma and how confronting our fears accepting vulnerability and cultivating self-compassion are crucial steps to healing.

The Unspoken Cost of Pain

Childhood trauma comes in different forms, ranging from abuse and emotional abuse, to physical and sexual assault. No matter what the nature of the incident it leaves a lasting impression on our minds. The traces of these can be carried on our bodies.

In silence, we carry on grieving for a long time, hoping they will heal or we will forget. The truth is that traumas left untreated have an ability of coming back and affecting us and in ways we don't ever be aware of.

The power of Face Our Fears

Face our fears can be the initial and most daunting way to recover from traumas of childhood. Fears can manifest as depression, anxiety or a general anxiety. There is the fear of being judged of other people, the opening of past wounds as well as the intense emotional reactions that surface in the face of our history. However, facing the fears we have is similar to turning on a bright light in the dark it allows us to look at the events in our lives clearly and allows us to proceed with a clear goal.

Recognizing the pain

The process of acknowledging the trauma we endured when we were children can be a sigh of relief. We have to revisit those memories, and remember our vulnerability and the fear that the feeling of vulnerability and hurt. But, by doing this it helps us to validate our personal memories. We remember that we weren't blameless, but simply victims of situations outside our influence. It is essential to acknowledge this when getting out of the trap of the trauma.

Freedom of Truth Liberation of Truth

The sharing of our experiences with other people (trusted family members, friends and therapists is an act of self-confidence that is incredibly freeing. If we are honest with ourselves it allows us to let the past's grip on our lives. It is a way to break the chain of silence that surrounded our history and give ourselves the opportunity to be heard, seen and listened to. Through these times of vulnerability We discover the strength and determination of our lives.

Sharing Your Story About the trauma of your childhood

The Appeal of Vulnerability

Being vulnerable isn't a sign of weakness, it is an affirmation of the humanity of us. It's an acknowledgement of the fact that we're imperfect creatures who are affected by our past experiences. If we speak up about the trauma of childhood, we allow other people to join us to share our experiences, both the pain as well as our triumphs. By sharing our experiences we build relationships that are more than superficial and help to establish the basis to heal properly.

Breaking Down Walls

In many cases, the concept of vulnerability can be difficult since it requires tearing down the barriers we've constructed to defend ourselves. The walls we've built were a the aftermath of our trauma in childhood, as a defence mechanism designed to protect ourselves from harm. But as we mature the walls may make it difficult to establish real relationships and to find true joy.

Connection and Empathy

If we are willing to be vulnerable and openly share our struggles to others, we can open the doors to compassion and connections. We realize that we're not alone in our struggle when we share our stories. Other people may also have personal stories of suffering as well as healing. And by telling our stories and allowing others to share theirs, we can create an environment that allows for understanding and mutual support.

The Love We deserve

The practice of self-compassion is a vital element of talking about the trauma of childhood. Self-compassion means giving ourselves the same respect and compassion as we would show a loved one who is suffering. Self-compassion can help us take care of ourselves when we travel through the rugged landscape of

healing.

The Letting Off Self-Blam

Children who suffer from trauma are often left feeling a feelings of self-blame. It is possible to think that we brought the hurt on ourselves, or be in a position to avoid the pain. Self-compassion can help us let go of the burdensome thoughts and realize that we don't have any responsibility.

to the actions of other people.

Nurturing our Inner Child

When we begin our recovery process, it is important to be a good parent to our child - the younger self that was affected by the experience. The child inside us needs love, affection and recognition. Self-compassion allows us to offer the necessary support to recover from the scars of our history.

Chapter 9: The Three Parts Of Trauma

In order to heal from traumas of childhood It is essential to comprehend the three elements of trauma: the incident as well as the experience and the impact. The following chapter sheds the light on these elements and provide valuable information on the path to healing.

Trauma isn't just a singular thing; it's an interplay of different events as well as experiences and consequences that affect the lives of all. In this section we'll explore the complex web of trauma and break it into three key parts: the event itself as well as the experience associated with the incident, and finally the effects. Through analyzing these elements it will provide valuable insights to the path of recovery and healing.

The Event is the Catalyst of Trauma

The initial aspect of trauma involves the event itself, the trigger that creates the conditions for the next psychological and emotional anxiety. The events that lead to concussions tend to be unplanned and often overwhelming. Concussions can result from a range of events including physical injuries to emotional hurts, acts of violence, as well as natural catastrophes. The thing that makes a tragedy is the potential for it to shake the illusion of security and safety.

Unexpected and overwhelming

Tragic events are characterised by their sudden, overwhelming characteristics. They frighten us and leave us feeling a sense of insecurity. These are the moments when our lives may change in a way that is irreparably.

Loss of Control

A common theme in traumatic experiences is the sense of loss of control. It doesn't matter if it's an accident in the car or an attack on a person the feeling of insecurity is one of the most common signs of trauma.

Loss of control could cause deep wounds and affect the feeling of being in control.

Variability of Traumatic Event

These events can be highly personal and can differ from one individual to individual. If one person finds it traumatic is not for another. The circumstances surrounding the incident, your the personal story, and mechanisms for coping play part in the effect.

Learning Trauma and the Three Parts of Trauma

The Emotional Resonance of the Event
Emotional Resonance

The other component of trauma is experiencing of the incident, and the emotional and emotional response that it triggers. This is when the true extent of the trauma is apparent when our bodies and minds react to the trauma-inducing event.

Fight, Fly or Freeze

The body's response is often "fight, flight, or freeze" when we experience trauma. It's an instinctual response created to aid us in surviving when confronted with threats. But, it can turn out to be unadaptive after trauma and leaves us feeling heightened alertness or a sense of numbness.

Memory Invasion

One of the main characteristics that trauma sufferers have is recurrence of disturbing memories. They can pop up in unexpected ways making their way into our thoughts and our sleep. They serve as constantly a memory of the experience and may trigger depression, anxiety and perhaps post-traumatic stress disorders (PTSD).

Emotional Stress

Trauma can bring forth an array of emotions. Fear, anger as well as shame, guilt and even sadness are often a part of the event. The overwhelming emotion makes it challenging to handle the events that follow.

The Effect: Permanent Damage and Scars

The last aspect of the trauma process is the impact the trauma has on us. It is here that the real consequences of the trauma emerge because it causes permanent scars that alter how we see ourselves and our surroundings.

Altered Belief Systems

The trauma of life is capable of shifting our fundamental beliefs. It is possible to believe that our world is in danger or that the people we trust are not trustworthy or that we're completely flawed. This belief can affect the way we interact and make decisions within our daily lives.

Mechanisms for Coping

As a result of stress, people tend to develop strategies for coping -- ways to deal with the distress and emotional trauma. While certain coping strategies may be adaptive, like seeking out therapy or help but others are not so adaptive for example, like addiction or self-harm.

Influence on relationships

The effects of trauma can be profoundly detrimental to the ability of us to build and sustain good relationships. The issues of trust, emotional distance and difficulties with intimacy are typical issues those who have suffered trauma are faced with.

Three Parts: The Interplay of the Three Parts

It is vital to realize the fact that all three components of trauma are interrelated. The way the incident is experienced affects the way it is experienced, and influences the long-lasting consequences. Knowing how this interaction plays out is essential to the process of healing.

Chapter 10: Childhood Have On Adults

Discover how traumas from childhood shape your adulthood. From the emotional burden to relationships patterns, we'll look at the impact of trauma on your everyday life. Childhood is the time full of wonder and excitement However, for certain people, it is a time of the trauma of childhood that casts a lengthy shadow over the adulthood. The traumas and experiences from childhood may have severe lasting impacts on the lives of adults. In this section we'll look at how trauma from childhood influences our lives, from carrying our emotional baggage, to influencing our pattern of relationships. We will also explore how knowing the impact of these traumas is an essential step in the healing process. The emotional baggage we carry

Childhood trauma can leave us with an emotional burden, which can last until adulthood. The emotional scars we carry can manifest through a variety of ways and influence the way we live and make decisions.

A lingering anxiety and fear

Traumas can trigger increased levels of fear and anxiety which persist throughout adulthood. It can appear to be more terrifying, and people experiencing trauma are always on guard, anticipating the worst at every turn.

Low self-esteem and low self-worth

The trauma of childhood can have a profound impact on confidence in ourselves and our worth. People who have suffered from trauma may experience feelings of guilt, shame, or feeling of worthlessness. They believe that they're imperfect or unworthy of happiness and love.

It is difficult to express emotions.

The majority of people who suffer from childhood trauma have trouble expressing their feelings. Some may have learned to hide their feelings in order to deal with those difficult experiences. In adulthood, this psychological suppression can limit the ability of people to build profound and lasting connections with other people.

The patterns of relationships shaped by trauma

The bonds we build as a result of the children are often influenced by our experiences as adulthood. Trauma from childhood can create certain patterns in relationships which may be both rewarding and challenging.

Trust Problems

Problems with trust are one of the main effects of childhood trauma and relationships. People who have suffered from trauma may be unable to believe in others due to fear of the possibility of being abandoned or having their trust violated. It can cause difficulties with forming bonds of trust and keeping good relationships.

Codependency

A few survivors of trauma from childhood can develop codependent tendencies. It can be manifested as an intense need for validation and acceptance from other people, usually at the expense their health. Relationships with codependent partners can be filled with imbalance and dysfunction.

Repeating Traumatic patterns

The phenomenon is known by the term "repetition compulsion," individuals who were victims of trauma as kids might unconsciously search for relationships or circumstances that are similar to their trauma-related experiences. This could lead to the cycle of re-traumatization because they are in the same situations.

harmful dynamics.

Strategies for Coping That Last

A lot of people develop strategies for coping to cope with childhood trauma, which can be beneficial in the early years of their lives. But, the same methods of coping can become ineffective as they grow older.

Substance Abuse

A few survivors resort to drug use to ease the pain of their lives. The use of alcohol, drugs as well as other addictive behavior can offer temporary relief, but they can also increase the effects of trauma.

Self-Harm

Self-harm is a different coping strategy that may persist throughout adulthood. People may resort to self-destructive behavior to deal with the overwhelming emotion and to regain their sense of control.

Avoidance and isolation

Isolation and avoidance can be the most common coping methods for people who are survivors of trauma in childhood. People may avoid social activities and avoid situations which trigger memories creating feelings of isolation and anxiety.

The Effect on Parenting

In the case of children who have suffered trauma, who later become parents, their effects may extend to the parenting style and how they interact with their children.

Parents who are overprotective

Certain survivors might become protective parents, trying to protect their children from danger or anxiety. Although they may be well-meaning, it can affect their child's growth and self-confidence.

Trouble bonding with children

Trauma may also hinder the ability of survivors to connect and bond emotionally with children. A distance of emotional connection to their not resolved trauma may affect the capacity of their attachment to be healthy.

Reversing The Cycle of Trauma

Recognizing how childhood trauma affects adulthood is the initial step in stopping the cycle of misery and dysfunction. Being aware of these patterns will allow those who have suffered to take proactive steps towards healing and living happier, healthier lives.

Needing professional help

Counseling and therapy are valuable sources for those who have experienced childhood trauma. A trained therapist can assist those who have suffered trauma to build healthy strategies for coping and deal with relationship issues.

Chapter 11: Recognizing The Signs Of Trauma

The marks left by childhood traumas can remain under the surface, quietly impacting our lives in surprising ways. In order to begin an emotional healing process it is crucial to be aware of the indicators of trauma that is not resolved. In this section we'll assist you to discern these warning signs and help you to recover from the scars of the previous.

The Long-lasting Impact of Childhood Trauma

Childhood trauma usually leaves long-lasting and lasting marks on our emotional and psychological wellbeing. They can show up across a variety of aspects of our lives. They are often unseen until we look at our past experiences and actions.

Perpetually intrusive thoughts

A common symptom of an unresolved trauma can be recurring disturbing thoughts or memories relating to the trauma. They can encroach upon your day-to-day life and cause anxiety and stress. It is possible that you will relive your experience as though the same thing happened.

Nightmares and Flashbacks

The flashbacks that you experience, which are vivid and painful thoughts of the traumatic incident are also signs of an unresolved trauma. Similar to nightmares that center around trauma can cause insomnia and cause you to feel anxious and distraught upon awakening.

Avoidance and Numbing

Behaviors of avoidance are another sign of trauma that is not fully resolved. The person may choose to either consciously or involuntarily avoid people, situations and places that trigger you of your trauma. The avoidance of situations, people, or places can be

can be extended to other numbing activities that include substance abuse and eating too much for relief from emotional distress.

Emotional Dysregulation

Instability in regulating emotions, or difficulties with managing and expressing emotion can be a symptom of traumas that are not fully resolved. It is possible that you are experiencing extreme emotions that are hard to control and can result in eruptions of anger, sadness or even stress.

Hypervigilance

The survivors of trauma often experience hypervigilance, a elevated state of alertness as well as an anxiety. It is possible to constantly monitor your surroundings for signs of danger even though there's any immediate threat.

Emotional Numbness and Detachment

A few people experience emotional feelings of numbness, or a feeling of detachment at opposite sides on the spectrum. It can be manifested as feelings of emptyness and a failure to connect with other people emotionally or feel a sense that you are removed from your feelings.

Disturbed Self-Perception

The trauma of childhood may alter the self-image, leading to self-deflection and a negative view of yourself as well as the value you have.

A low self-esteem

An indication of an unresolved trauma is a lower self-esteem. There are times when you feel guilt, shame, or feeling of worthlessness. You may believe that you are unworthy of happiness and love.

Self-Destructive Behaviours

Traumas that are not resolved can trigger self-destructive behaviours as a means to deal with emotional distress. This could include self-harm and substance abuse as well as unsafe activities.

Relations Challenges

Unresolved trauma could affect relations. There are times when you struggle to form or maintaining healthy bonds with your loved ones because of trust issues, physical distance or difficulties dealing with the intimacy.

Health and Physical Symptoms

Traumas that are not resolved can result in physical signs as well as health problems.

Chronic Pain

Certain people who have unresolved trauma can suffer from chronic pain usually a result of the tension and psychological stress that result from the trauma.

Sleep Disturbances

The presence of sleep disorders, such as insomnia or sleep disturbances, could be a sign of unresolved trauma. Flashbacks and nightmares may hinder restful sleeping.

Stress-related health problems that are related to stress

The stress that is a result of unresolved traumas can cause numerous health issues, such as heart disease, autoimmune diseases as well as compromised immune function.

Strategies for Coping That Last

The survivors of trauma from childhood often create coping strategies to get through the trauma. Though these strategies to cope might have been needed but they may become unadaptive as they grow older.

Avoidance and isolation

Behaviors of avoidance, like being isolated from other people or avoidance of situations that trigger you, are common indicators of a trauma unresolved. This can hamper the ability of you to fully participate with the world around you.

Self-Medicating

The self-medicating process of using substances or similar addictive behaviours is yet another way of coping which can last into adulthood. The behaviors offer short-term relief but can actually increase the trauma that is underlying.

Control and Perfectionism

Many people deal with the trauma they are struggling with by looking for control and perfection. It is possible to strive for total control over the environment, or even develop perfectionist tendencies in hopes of preventing the occurrence of trauma in the future by doing so.

Chapter 12: The Seven Healing Stages

Recovering from childhood trauma can be a long process that is unfolds over time. Each step is crucial for inner peace, healing and change. In this chapter, we will look at seven areas of healing from trauma from childhood From denial to healing giving guidance and tips to anyone who are embarking on this journey of courage.

Stage 1: Denial

The initial stage of healing following trauma in childhood usually is a period of the process of denial. When this happens, victims are likely to try to conceal or reduce their experiences from the past. This is a defensive way to ward off the overwhelming feelings and thoughts that are associated with trauma.

The Signs of Denialism

The avoidance of talking or pondering about the painful incident. Downplaying the seriousness of the incident

Reducing the effects of trauma to one's daily life

Engaging in distractions, or other using numbing techniques to protect yourself from the emotional trauma

Stage 2: Awareness

Awareness is an important moment in the process of healing. It is the moment when one acknowledges the presence of the incident as well as the impact it has on one's living. The process can be difficult since it demands confronting the unpleasant truths about the history.

The signs of awareness

Recognizing the psychological and emotional impacts of the trauma that the event took place and wasn't an individual's responsibility. Looking for knowledge and information about the effects of trauma the desire to confront and overcome the experience

3. Acceptance

Acceptance is the process by which people come to terms with their experiences. Accepting the reality of what transpired and the ability to mourn the hurt and loss that comes with the time.

Signatures of Acceptance

Expression of emotions connected to the emotional trauma such as anger, sadness, and sorrow Letting go of guilt and self-blame

Building a self-compassion, forgiveness and acceptance. to the notion of asking for help and assistance

The 7 Healing Stages from Childhood Trauma

Stage 4: Understanding

Understanding is an essential step on the path to healing. This involves understanding the causes of trauma, their effect on the way one thinks and behaviours, and the way the experience has affected one's lifestyle.

The signs of Understanding

Investigating the root cause and underlying causes of the trauma, and recognizing how the experience has affected one's perception of oneself and their relationships. Understanding the connection between previous experiences and current difficulties Engaging in self reflection and therapy to gain a deeper knowledge

Stage 5 Stage 5: Grieving

The process of grieving is one that helps survivors let go the emotions and pain that have been that have been buried for so long. The process involves grieving the loss that comes with experience, such as losing innocence and security and faith.

Expressions of grief

Experimenting with intense emotions like sadness, anger and depression. Allowing oneself to cry and grieve

Looking for help from a counselor or a support group for grieving. Having moments of relief and catharsis from emotional stress

Step 6: Tolerance

It isn't about allowing the acts of those who created the tragedy; rather, it's about getting rid of the hold of resentment and anger that make survivors stuck in their past. The process of forgiveness is deeply personal and unique process.

The Signs of Forgiveness

Understanding that forgiveness is an act of kindness to self and not to one's perpetrator. Giving up the need for justice or revenge. Work towards letting go of the self-blame and guilt. an inner peace and relaxation by forgiveness

Chapter 13: The 3 Steps To Beating Childhood Trauma

Resolving childhood trauma is a difficult, yet deeply transformative experience. This chapter will discuss the three fundamental steps for recuperating and healing from childhood trauma: understanding the damage, practicing patience and seeking professional aid. These simple steps are the ways to get on the road towards healing and rebuilding your life.

Step 1: Confirm the trauma

Recognizing trauma is the primary process to heal. This means acknowledging the presence of trauma from childhood, comprehending the impact it has on your life and acknowledging that recovery is necessary and achievable.

Accepting the Trauma

Face the Pain: Accept that you have experienced trauma in childhood. It could mean the revisiting of painful emotions and memories that can be overwhelming however it is vital to heal. Confirm Your Experience: Be aware that the trauma you experienced is real and true. The issue is not yours and you're not the only one in the struggle.

Stopping the Silence: break the silence that surrounds your trauma. Talk about your experience with loved ones, trusted relatives or with an therapist. Being honest can be an effective act of freedom.

Understanding the Implications

Self-Reflection: Reflect on your own actions to discover how your experience affected your thoughts as well as your behavior and relationship. Consider how the trauma may have had an impact on your decisions in the present.

Find your Unmask Coping Mechanisms. ways to cope that you've used to cope with the trauma.

Whether adaptive or non-adaptive. Learning these coping strategies is essential for the healing process.

Recognizing the Need to Healing

Accept Healing as a Need Accept that healing isn't an option but rather a necessity. You have the right to get better and to find the peace you need after suffering the trauma of your life.

Be resilient and hopeful: cultivate faith and develop resilience. Believe that healing is achievable as many have discovered a way towards healing.

Step 2: Take Time for Youself

The process of healing from trauma in childhood is a journey that demands patience, perseverance as well as self-compassion. It is essential to be patient to yourself while you face the difficulties of healing.

Three Steps to Surmonting Childhood Trauma

Let the Healing Process Begin

There are no fixed timelines: Be aware that healing does not happen in a linear fashion There aren't time frames that can be fixed. Every person's story is different and the rate of recovery differs from individual to.

Make realistic expectations: Try to avoid creating unrealistic expectations of yourself. The process of healing can be difficult and may include setbacks as well as times of vulnerability that are completely normal.

Do self-compassion exercises

Be Kind to Yourself You should treat yourself with the same understanding and compassion that you'd show a person suffering. Self-compassion can be a very effective instrument for recovery. Take on the challenge of negative self-talk. Pay attention to negative self-talk and self-criticism. Replace self-criticism by self-affirmation and positive reinforcement.

Self-care and self-care

Make Self-Care a priority: Adopt self-care strategies that improve physical, emotional, as well as wellbeing in the mind. These could be mindfulness practices meditation, relaxation techniques, exercises and a healthy way of life.

Develop a supportive and safe environment. Create a positive family of friends and loved ones who can understand the journey you are on and offer an area of healing that is secure.

Step 3: Get professional assistance

Professional help can be an essential step to overcome childhood trauma. Counselors and therapists who are trained can give guidance, help and interventions based on evidence to help to heal.

The benefits of professional help

Expert guidance Counselors and therapists possess experience in dealing with trauma and are able to assist you in your healing process. They provide proven techniques that can be that are tailored to your individual demands.

The Safe Space offers the security and privacy needed for you to talk about your experiences and emotions and devise strategies to cope.

Validation and support Therapists can confirm your experience and offer emotional assistance. They will help you overcome the negative thoughts and build self-confidence that is more positive.

Therapies for different types

The therapy is trauma-informed and is designed specifically to meet the specific demands of survivors of trauma. It is focused on the safety of people, trust, freedom as well as empowerment, cooperation, and collaboration.

Cognitive-Behavioral therapy (CBT) CBT is a therapy that can aid you to identify and alter negative thoughts and behavior patterns associated with trauma.

Eye Movement Desensitization Reprocessing (EMDR) is a type of therapy that is a specific therapy which can assist in the processing of painful memories as well as reduce the emotional burden.

Support Groups

Peer Support: You might want to consider getting involved in support groups for survivors of trauma. The groups provide a feeling of community, knowledge, and the chance to gain knowledge from other's experience.

Online Communities: Besides the support groups in person There are a myriad of internet-based communities as well as forums that survivors of trauma are able to connect and discuss their experiences.

Chapter 14: The Consequences Of Not Recovering

Childhood trauma leaves a shadow that may last into adulthood, affecting every aspect of your daily life. Failure to overcome childhood traumas can create a vicious cycle of suffering and limits. This chapter will discuss the devastating consequences of not healing. We will highlight the

important to break free of the chains that tie your to the old. It is vital to break free from the chains that bind you to your past. Cycle of Pain

1. Repeating patterns

Traumas from childhood that have not been addressed can lead to the repeating of certain routines. It can manifest in a variety of ways, which include:

In the course of reliving toxic relationships, survivors might not realize they are seeking friendships that reflect their trauma events' patterns, which can lead to more harm and stress. Self-Sabotage: A lack of resolution to trauma may result in self-defeating behavior which hinders you from achieving your goals and achieving your potential to the maximum.

Coping Mechanisms: Unnatural strategies for coping, like self-harm or addiction to substances are likely to persist and increase the emotional suffering.

2. Emotional Turbulence

The inability to heal from traumas of childhood may result in a perpetual feeling of anxiety. The symptoms can include:

Unresolved Grief: Grief as well as depression that are a result of trauma could remain unprocessed which can lead to a long-lasting sadness and depression.

Stress and anxiety: Afraid and anxiety could be chronic and make your quest for peace and security the daily routine difficult.

Resentment and Anger: Insufferable anger and resentment focused outwards or inwards it can affect your relationships as well as affect your overall health.

3. Negative Self-Beliefs

Trauma from childhood often creates beliefs about self that are negative and persist throughout adulthood. This includes:

A lack of self-esteem: Some survivors have a strong self-esteem issue, leading to missed opportunities as well as unfulfilled potential.

Self-Blame: A lot of trauma survivors take responsibility for their own actions and carry on feelings of shame and guilt.

Insecurity: The difficulty of confidence in oneself or others could hinder the development of strong relationships as well as an underlying sense of security.

Limitations of Life

1. Personal Growth Stunted

Traumas from childhood that have not been addressed may hinder the personal development and growth of a person in different ways:

Uncertainty Lack of confidence can be a result of weakened confidence due to self-defeating beliefs caused by the trauma of your past, limiting your capacity to be risk-averse and seek opportunities. Refraining from Challenges A fear of failing or rejection may result in avoiding difficulties and a refusal to leave your comfortable area.

Affordability: You can restrict your activities and interests in order to avoid feeling a sense confidence in yourself or fear of judgement.

2. Interference with respect to relationships

Childhood trauma may be detrimental in your capacity to build and sustain healthy relationships.

Trust issues: Having trust in others can be difficult, which leads to problems in building close relationships and creating the bonds of intimacy.

Emotional Distance: Emotional separation and separation can stop the person from having genuine relationships with other people.

A few survivors might be codependent, depending on other people for validation and self-esteem.

3. The Workplace

Traumas that are not addressed can negatively impact your career and professional lives through the following methods:

Troubled Concentration: Insane thoughts or emotional stress may affect your ability focus and be productive at work or in school.

Insufficient Opportunities: Lack of self-confidence, and worry about failing can result in missed opportunities to grow professionally.

A lack of ambition: Limitations caused by trauma limit your potential and limit your ability to pursue important objectives.

Its Impact on Physical Health

Childhood traumas that are not addressed can be detrimental to the physical condition:

Chronic Stress: strain caused by unresolved traumas can cause a depletion of the immunity, heart problems and an increased chance of developing chronic illness. Ineffective Coping Strategies Addiction to substances and self-destructive behavior can lead to a worsening of physical health concerns.

Sleep Sleep disturbances like insomnia, nightmares and sleep apnea may also affect your physical wellbeing.

The Vicious Cycle

Failure to deal with childhood trauma creates an unending cycle where suffering leads to more pain.

Denial and Avoidance: Constant rejection and avoidance of the trauma-related concerns hinders the healing process. Self-beliefs that are reinforced: negative self-beliefs reinforce the effects of trauma are exacerbated. Stagnation: Mental, emotional stagnation of the personal and emotional are commonplace.

Unlocking the Cycle

Knowing the effects of not healing through childhood trauma can be an effective motivator to embark in the process of the road to recovery. The process of breaking free of limitations and pain requires determination, self-compassion and an investment in your health.

Needing professional help

Therapy and counseling Therapy and Counseling: The assistance of a professional is essential to address unresolved trauma. Therapy is a secure and supportive setting to process trauma as well as creating strategies for coping.

Informed Trauma Care: Find caregivers who have been trained in addressing the particular demands of survivors of trauma.

Self-Care, Self-Compassion and Self-Compassion

It is important to prioritize self-care. Self-care techniques including relaxation, mindfulness as well as physical exercise, will help to reduce stress and boost health and well-being. Learn to replace criticism of yourself with self-compassion. Give yourself a hug and realize that healing is an ongoing process that involves the occasional ups and downs.

Build Relationships That Support Each Other

Connect to Others: Create an online community of family and friends who are able to offer empathy and support.

Take part in support groups: You might consider joining support groups specifically for trauma survivors in order to network with those who've had similar experiences.

Be a part of healing

Create realistic goals: Establish realistic goals for your healing process. Be grateful for small successes throughout the process.

Be Persistent: Recovering from trauma from childhood isn't always simple, but persistence is essential. Be persistent, regardless of challenges.

Chapter 15: Looking For Greater Happiness And Health

Recovering from childhood trauma not just about conquering the pain, but rather about regaining the happiness, health and completeness hidden by the darkness from the past In this chapter, we will discuss the self-care strategies, resilience-building techniques as well as ways to restore your strength, helping you to live a happier, more healthy life.

Self-Care and Healing Practices

Self-care is an essential component of overcoming childhood trauma. The practices you practice provide nourishment to your mind, body as well as your soul. They provide the resilience and strength needed to achieve optimal wellbeing and joy.

1. Mindfulness and meditation

Mindfulness: Develop mindfulness by engaging in exercises like deep breathing, meditation or even yoga. The practice of mindfulness helps you remain focused, reduce stress and lessen anxiety. Meditation: Regular sessions of meditation help to improve emotional equilibrium, increase self-awareness, as well as create the feeling of being calm and peace.

2. Health and Physical Health and Exercise

Regular exercise: Regularly work out to improve mood, decrease anxiety, and boost overall health. Exercise produces endorphins that can be natural mood boosters. A healthy diet: Provide your body by eating a healthy nutrition-rich diet. Nutritional balance is essential for both physical and mental well-being.

3. Sleep Hygiene

Set up a routine: Develop the habit of a regular sleep schedule, and ensure you are practicing good sleep hygiene. Sleeping well is crucial to heal physical and emotional.

Limit screen time: Cut down on the time spent on screen before bed to enhance sleep quality. Screens' blue lights can interfere with the circadian rhythms.

4. Expression of Creativity

Arts and Crafts: Discover artistic outlets like painting, writing or playing music to express your feelings, and to release any bottled-up emotions.

Journaling: Use a journal for reflection on your life experiences to track progress and gain insight on your journey to healing.

Building Resilience

Resilience refers to the capacity to recover from the hardship and excel even in the face of hardships. Resilience is crucial to recovery and for embracing well-being and happiness.

1. Create A Help Network

Make Connections with Others: Create bonds with your family and friends and support group. The sharing of your experience and the receiving of assistance can help build the resilience.

Get professional help Take advantage of counseling or therapy to build your resilience and mental resilient.

2. Positive Self-Talk

Change Negative Beliefs and Challenge Negative Thoughts Replace negative self-talk with affirmations that are positive. Remember your strengths and growth.

Develop Self-Compassion: be compassionate to yourself, particularly when you are facing difficult moments. Self-compassion builds resilience and improves mental well-being.

3. Emotion Regulation

Recognize Triggers: You can determine emotional triggers and devise strategies for managing emotions.

Healthier Coping Methods to Replace unhealthy strategies for coping with stress by using healthy ones like meditation, exercise as well as deep breathing.

4. Goal Setting and Accomplishment

Make Realistic Goals: Create realistic goals to help you on your healing process. Honor your achievements throughout the process.

Recognize Progress: Celebrate your achievements, regardless of the size. Each step will be a win in your goal to be healthy and happy.

Reclaiming Your Power

In order to regain control, it's about taking the reins of your lifestyle and making decisions in line with your needs and beliefs. It's an essential step to greater health, happiness and completeness.

1. Boundaries

Make the boundaries of your personal and professional relationships. They protect your mental health and your freedom.

Make a habit of saying no. Learn the art of saying no when it is necessary, and prioritizing your requirements and self-care with no guilt.

2. Self-Advocacy

Make a Statement: Advocate for your desires and needs when it comes to relationships, work and in your community. Your voice is important, and you are entitled to be heard.

Get Support: If you have difficulty with your self-talk, you should seek help from an therapist or counselor in order for help in developing these skills.

3. Your Life Vision and Goals

Definition of Your Vision Establish your long-term vision of life as well as objectives. Understanding what you are looking for can help you make the right choices as well as your actions.

Design a Plan: Make an action plan for achieving your objectives. Divide them into achievable steps and milestones.

4. Self-Compassion and Forgiveness

Self-Compassion: Continue to practice self-compassion and self forgiveness. Be accepting of your shortcomings and give yourself the same kindness that you would give a person. In the process of healing and heal, think about forgiving the people that caused the trauma. It is an effective way to let go of the past's influence over your current situation.

Connecting to Joy

Recovering from childhood traumas opens the way to finding the joy and satisfaction that comes from it. Engage in activities and routines that will bring happiness to your daily life.

1. Discover joy in the smallest Moments

Develop a habit of gratitude: Be grateful to the tiny joys of the world. Journals of gratitude helps you to focus on the good aspects of your day.

Be mindful Take note of the beautiful moments of your day--the sunshine's warm glow, the smiles of family and friends, or the aroma of a favourite food.

2. Explore your Passions and Hobbies

Connect with your Passions: Recall your childhood interests or discover the new areas of interest that can spark excitement and ingenuity.

Engage in Hobbies: Participate with hobbies and other activities which bring pleasure and satisfaction. Make time for your interests on a regular basis.

3. Connection and Love

Nurture Relationships: Increase your relationships with your loved ones. Be sure to share laughter, love and memorable memories.

Self-Love: Build a solid feeling of self-love and acceptance. Accept your own inherent value of happiness and love.

Chapter 16: Finding Solace In Faith

Faith can be a significant source of comfort, strength and healing for a lot of those who are recovery from childhood trauma. This chapter we'll examine the healing to be found in faith. It will highlight how your faith in God could be a source of hope, and also the catalyst to change.

The power of Faith in Healing

1. The source of Comfort

Divine Presence Faith gives a feeling of God's presence and provides comfort and peace during times of stress.

Prayer: Praying can provide comfort, and allows the person to let their feelings out and receive direction from an inner source.

2. Framework for Meaning: A Framework for Meaning

Finding Meaning: Faith can help you discover meaning and a purpose for your life, even in the suffering and pain of trauma in childhood.

Understanding the Causes of Suffering: Many religions and traditions provide insight on the causes of suffering as well as the potential that one can grow through the challenges.

3. The Path for Forgiveness

To forgive: Faith often emphasizes the necessity of forgiving the other and for oneself. It can be an important stage in healing.

The release of resentment will relieve the burden of resentment and free your from the shackles of bitterness and anger.

Inspiring Your Faith

1. Connection through prayer

Daily Prayer: Develop an everyday prayer routine to build a strong bond to God. Utilize this time to voice your emotions, ask for advice, and experience the peace within yourself. Prayer to heal: Make particular prayers to heal and asking God's guidance as well as support on your path towards completeness.

2. Spiritual Community

Go to services If you're any religious beliefs, participating in religious services or gatherings could give the feeling of being part of a community as well as help.

Join Supportive Groups: Check out support groups, or groups that focus on healing and resolving trauma.

3. Meditation and reflection

Meditation: Integrate meditation and your faith in meditating on holy texts or ideas that are related to healing and resilience.

Journaling: Make use of journaling to contemplate your spiritual journey, write down your prayer requests, and keep track of your growth.

4. Find For Guidance

Spiritual counselor or leader You may want to seek guidance from a spiritual counsellor or a religious leader that can offer guidance and advice that is specific to the faith you hold. The Interfaith Explorer: Discover various perspectives from different faiths regarding healing and recovery in order to develop more understanding of the spiritual.

The Power of Strength in adversity

1. A Story of Job Story of Job

Resilience and Faith through faith: The Bible story of Job emphasizes the importance of resilience in the confronting of hardship by faith and trusting in God.

An Inspirational Source Job's story of perseverance and ultimately recovery may inspire people who are facing hardships.

2. Stories of Transformation

Stories of healing: Find out stories and testimonials of those who've gained healing and found solace in their faith.

Role Models: Look for the role models within your religious community that have overcome hardship or adversity and used their stories as sources of motivation.

Incorporating Spirituality in the process of healing

1. Mind Body Spirit Connection

Holistic Healing: Be aware of that your body, mind, as well as your spirituality in this healing procedure.

Balancing Practices: Incorporate spiritual practices along with other types of healing like meditation, therapy, or self-care.

2. The cultivation of hope

Hope as a healing force Know the potential of hope as a healing force which will help you get through tough moments.

Hope and Faith The two are closely interspersed. The faith you have can foster hopes, while hope may give you the courage to keep going on your path to recovery.

The Challenges and the Questions

1. The Struggles and Doubts

Doubt as a Natural Process Understanding that doubt and uncertainty are normal aspects of spirituality and faith. These are not detrimental to the connection you have to God.

Looking for answers By way of prayer, meditation and conversations with spiritual advisors, consider the questions you have and your doubts.

2. Theodicy

"The Problem of Suffering Theodicy explores the theological basis of the reason why we suffer. Be engaged with this topic in your religious tradition for answers and insight. Conciliating Faith: Focus on reconciling your faith and the realities of your personal trauma. Get help from spiritual experts or theologians that specialize in this field. The pages in "Healing the Inner Child: A Woman's Guide to Overcoming Childhood Trauma," we took a deep trip that revealed the way between darkness and pain towards healing and completeness. Through this book we examined the complexity that come with childhood traumas, its effects on the quality of your life and the transformational power of healing.

The healing process you have undergone is testimony to your strength as well as your strength and determination. For a woman who been confronted by the darkness of your past, you've embarked in a journey of self-discovery, self-compassion and self-discovery. This is the last chapter, let's consider the main lessons in this book:

1. Then, recognizing the trauma

Accepting the fact that you have suffered from childhood trauma is the initial bold step to recovery. Sharing your story will free you from the burden of silence as well as shame and refusal. Keep in mind your experience is real as are your feelings true. There is no one else on this path, and the best part is that there is

strength in vulnerability.

2. Learning Trauma and the Three Parts of Trauma

The term "trauma" refers to the actual event as well as your perception of the experience, and the long-lasting impact it has in your life. Knowing these components can help you discover the root of your suffering and how it has changed your thoughts and actions. Knowing the three components of trauma is crucial to unravelling the web of the past.

3. The Effects of Childhood trauma on Adulthood

Childhood trauma deeply imprints. Talking about the experiences you've had can help you live your life to the fullest and can affect your mental health as well as your relationships and life. If you are aware of these effects and recognizing the effects, you will be able to remove and eliminate the barriers have been erected by trauma, opening your way to a better future.

4. Indicates a Trauma that has not been resolved

The aftermath of trauma that's not addressed is often invisible, yet powerful Indicators. The recognition of these signals of emotional reactivity self-sabotaging behavior, and relationships patterns -- allows you to face and heal from past hurts.

5. The 7 Healing Stages in Childhood Trauma

The journey to healing that began with childhood trauma is a series of seven stages of transformation, ranging from denial to flourishing. These stages offer a road map to your healing, providing advice and guidance to traverse the challenges of recovering.

6. The 3 Steps to Surmonting Childhood Trauma

Becoming aware of your trauma, maintaining patience with yourself as well as seeking help from a professional are the first three ways to heal from childhood trauma. This practical approach will enable you to manage your recovery journey and take back your life.

7. The consequences of Not Heiling

Knowing the effects of not dealing with the trauma of your childhood is an effective motivator to your journey to healing. It helps you understand the cycle of hurt as well as emotional turmoil and limitations that remain even when healing is not addressed and emphasizes the importance to find your way back.

8. Looking for greater health, happiness and Wellness

Your journey towards healing extends far beyond the simple absence of discomfort. The goal is to achieve optimal health, joy, and completeness. The practice of self-care, strategies for building resilience as well as the reclaiming of your potential are vital components of this endeavor.

9. Finding Solace within Faith

The faith of God can be a source of hope, and also an ally to strength and healing for people seeking support from the spiritual realm. Connecting to God can bring comfort in comfort, guidance, and peace when you are struggling with recovery.

Keep in mind that healing isn't an unending process, there isn't a set timeframe for the experience. It's a continuous constant exploration of your own self-discovery as well as growth and transformation. Accept the difficulties and rejoice in every victory, no matter how tiny it may seem.

www.ingramcontent.com/pod-product-compliance
Lightning Source LLC
Chambersburg PA
CBHW071443080526
44587CB00014B/1966